Seeing Laodicea

André Leferge

DEDICATION

This book was inspired by courageous and principled men, women and families of my acquaintance. It is my hope that their contributions to my life can be shared with you. In view of the injustice currently operating in some of their situations, locations and surnames have been omitted.

Mark and Fiona

Matt and Lori

Moise and Elizabeth

Norman and Grace

Raju and Ritah

Scott and Gayla

Steven and Helen

Stuart and Teresa

Tom and Ritah

ACKNOWLEDGEMENTS

Originality is such an impossible quality to verify, and it is likely that many others should be acknowledged here. However significant influences must be attributed to the following people. Some are authors, others friends.

Andy Lyde

Barney Coombs

Berni Comissiong

Gill Morgan

Jeremy Russell

Jill Lawson

John and Joyce Rawlings

Mark Arnold

Matt Summerfield

Miroslav Volf

Paul Stockley

Pete and Nicky Gilbert

Peter Greig

Peter Jeffrey

Rob Hudson

Scott and Gayla Congdon

Tom Wright

Vincent and Julie Oliver

Viv Grigg

With grateful thanks to Joey Lamb for her copywriting finesse.

CONTENTS

FOREWORD

After reading André's previous book, *Touching Smyrna*, I went to Burkina Faso and, in the process, met many of the real people who make up the characters in that story and it's continuation in the book you now hold. André captures the spirit of these real people on their journeys of transformation as they submit themselves to Christ. It was life–transforming for me to see the spiritual riches given to those who seek Jesus.

Perhaps troubling to the reader will be André's writing on the shallowness of many in the Church and on the life of physical oppression experienced by many followers of Christ around the world. Regarding the latter, the suffering of Christians because they are followers of Christ challenges the foundations of a faith grown in the protection of the western state. Our ability to protest a public corporation because we do not like how their policies line up with our faith starkly contrasts with the daily experience of a low caste "*untouchable*" in India with few state–guaranteed rights, perhaps none of which are protected in reality.

Likewise, how we make sense of the experience of Christians who are oppressed directly relates to the depth we will allow Jesus to take us. In a globalised economy, my decisions impact people around the world. Can I protest an organisation's domestic human resources decision without protesting that they make their profit through foreign exploited workers? These are topics that cut straight to our identity. No wonder we squirm.

André does not write to either of these topics to judge. Instead, I know it to be the opposite. He loves Jesus, he loves the Church, and he is uniquely positioned to bring to light to us a faith that is radically clinging to Jesus. We are challenged and instructed beautifully in a story form that makes accessible harsh realities and the truth of the Gospel. He would be delighted with our squirming, but exponentially more delighted if that squirming leads to a life more full of justice and righteousness.

i

I leave you with the two questions that confronted me as I read *Seeing Laodicea*. Where do I see myself in this story? How firmly am I clinging to Jesus, wherever that takes me?

May you be challenged and transformed to be more like Jesus.

Andy Lyde

(CEO, Amor Ministries)

———————————————

PREFACE

Welcome my friend, thank you for dropping by. Why are you here? I hope it may be because you are curious to find out what happens to the characters of my last book, *Touching Smyrna*. Sorry to leave things on a bit of a cliff edge for you. Let's see if over the next couple of hundred pages we can tidy them up a bit.

I call you my friend with no less presumption than you would employ if you used the term for me. You may not want to be my friend. That's no real problem to me. My friendship is not dependent on how you feel about me — it's an act of grace. But I digress. Let's get to the action.

You're just in time to observe a moment in history, which for one little girl is incredibly important. Be still with me for a little while and observe with hushed breath the wonder of her moment.

Her name is Daisy–June. Pretty isn't it? — just like her lovely smile. It's never shortened to Daisy; she is always Daisy–June, a name it is almost impossible to say without smiling.

Her mummy is holding Daisy–June's tiny hand, daddy grinning down at her as he turns the key and together they cross the threshold of her home for the first time.

There, it has happened and you got to see it unfold. Be respectful of this moment; allow it to enrich your soul.

Her home, that's what I said.

She has lived here for some time as a guest, but today the home is truly hers. Let me explain.

Around four years ago Alasdair and Nicole were fostering a teenage girl named Vicky. Vicky was in state care for the same reason that so many children enter the system; parenting so poor that it would be unjust and immoral to leave her in the hands of her parents.

Vicky became pregnant, and was helped through the various stages of her pregnancy by Alasdair and Nicole. When the time came for the birth Vicky chose Nicole to be with her, and Nicole was the second person to hold the tiny Daisy–June.

Responsibility can come hard to teenagers in care. Though she quickly and enthusiastically took to looking after Daisy–June, Vicky's resilience to the constant demands of a newborn baby quickly succumbed to the instincts of a survivor under pressure. She ran.

Alasdair and Nicole, at first dismayed by the turn of events that saw them exchange a foster child with a baby for a fostered newborn did what all amazing foster parents would. They placed their middle–aged lives on hold and attempted to help social services track down Vicky — all the while caring for Daisy–June as if she was their own.

Unsurprisingly bonding took place — and for the past four years they have loved this delightful baby girl as their own. Except that she was not their own; not until today. The courts, after much scrutiny regarding their suitability — including the records and behaviours of all their immediate family members and assessment of a viability of a claim on the child from Vicky — granted them adoption rights.

Alasdair and Nicole make a wonderful couple, living in a dream home. Their values are so beautiful and love so genuine that it is hard to comprehend the life journey they have shared to craft them. Starting at the bottom of the employment chain, they have worked their way up to roles of leadership and responsibility in social care and industry respectively. Their personal lives have been touched by both tragedy and critical illness of the greatest magnitude. Yet the overarching character trait of this dear couple is thankfulness.

Today for the first time, Daisy–June is theirs, and they are hers.

The state has relinquished its temporary responsibility regarding Daisy–June and they have stepped up to love her forever. Today she entered her home for the first time, which one day she will inherit, along with her new siblings; and you got to share the moment, my friend.

Will they live happily ever after? I doubt anyone does that. Life is complex and people are desperately difficult to understand and love. Relationships are really tricky, can be wrecked and can be remade, need investment and reinvestment. One thing I can say of this little family; they have made a great start and have every chance of enjoying wonderful loving relationships.

Alasdair and Nicole will have years to invest their values and principles in Daisy–June by demonstration and involvement. Before too long she will be her own person, owning none of their physical DNA but much of their spiritual and moral approach to life.

What did Daisy–June do to gain the love and affection Alasdair and Nicole ratified legally to permanence? Yelled her head off with demands and made mess — that's what! Hers is a story of grace; their grace.

So by a rather circuitous route we come to another story of grace; that given to Laodicea, an ancient Turkish church which receives what appears at first to be a rather chilling letter.

The canons of Scripture used by both the Eastern and Western churches as far back as AD 190 include the book of Revelation or as it is more traditionally called, 'the Apocalypse', which means more literally 'the drawing back of the curtain'.

The letter appears in this book and its contents purport to spell out both the feelings and the observations of the risen Jesus Christ. If the New Testament is to be believed then he is God in human form, crucified, risen from the dead, ascended and lives on, enthroned as the King of all Kings in the place from where all existence is governed. He is the one to whom all nations and their chosen rulers will give account.

So how is this letter both chilling and gracious? Let's deal with the chilling first. It describes a state of consciousness in which a stunning lack of self-awareness exists within the church.

> 'You say "I am rich, I have everything I want, I don't need anything!" And you don't realise you are poor and wretched, miserable and naked and blind.'

I'm not sure how one receives such a letter from such a writer? Perhaps in even starting to understand the contents we should first understand the motive.

A little bit like Alasdair and Nicole did with Daisy–June, God claims to have adopted this group of individuals. Quite literally legally adopted them, committing to permanent loving care, the conferring of family resources and inheritance rights.

But he's claimed to have done a bit more than that; by the infusion of himself in spirit he has formed them into a mutually interdependent group called a church and given them an exciting set of challenges to meet as they work with him on his causes of justice and right behaviour.

Fascinating then that they haven't really owned his values and this enormous gulf exists between how they see themselves and how he sees them. Chilling isn't it? Right up to the bit where the letter says

> 'I advise you to come and buy gold from me — gold that has been purified by fire, then you will be rich.'

What does the Christ, the author want? He wants his people to be rich. Not with the stuff they already have; he has described that as leaving them in an appalling state. He wants them to own true riches.

What can they be? How will they get them?

Well my friend, read on and let's see if we can't discover what he means; and as we do so, why not consider what you yourself are wearing?

André Leferge.

———————————————

1. NAKED

Benjamin Traoré had a problem. On one level, life was a beach and he was wearing the finest Bermuda shorts and Raybans on the strip. On another he lived with the constant searing pain of untreated emotional wounds.

This curious dichotomy had set about shrinking his ability to be thankful even in the most beautiful surroundings. And these surroundings were magnificent, even by Los Angeles standards. The Four Seasons Cabana restaurant, on the fourth floor offered a leafy poolside opulence that would be hard to match anywhere in the world. The food was exquisite, the crystal glasses spotless, the cutlery gleaming, the linen crisp and fresh. Waiters bustled respectfully and the air was gently filled with rich flawless jazz.

He would expect no less of a venue from his host, and settled back on his generous rump — shaped by too many lunches like this and filling his spacious chair.

His eyes widened in a warm, expertly simulated welcome as they fixed upon Joseph and Eve, pastors from Burkina Faso — one of

1

Seeing Laodicea

several nations in which he had spent many years delivering healthcare among the poor.

Introductions were made by the host, Casper Scales, a charismatic and highly successful young entrepreneur. He had an unusual ability to put his guests at ease. 'You found us! Well done, and right on time. Meet Benjamin; he's from your part of Africa!'

Eve and Joseph were a little late having struggled with the practicalities of finding then entering the grand establishment. They were smartly dressed and naturally handsome people but clearly ill at ease in this spotless, highly luxurious environment.

Casper ordered for everyone, effortlessly picking out some items from the "Indulgence" menu: seafood salad, smoked salmon wrap with the grilled asparagus; and a selection from the "Comfort" menu: que rico and burgers, of course. He insisted on dessert: the chocolate dipped frozen bananas with some sorbets and gelatos. The wine was a delightful Californian Pinot Grigio, chilled and bursting with tones of fresh melon and gooseberry. The Oudraogos drank San Pellegrino mineral water. They were teetotal but didn't find others' drinking offensive.

Casper asked Benjamin to give thanks to God for the food, which he did eloquently and thanklessly. Religion he could do; relationship he could not.

Casper's stylish and generous manner relaxed them wonderfully and soon they were laughing and delightedly exchanging shared experiences of places and even people, in his presence.

All agreed that the conference they'd just enjoyed had been challenging and invigorating, especially the keynote speaker from Pacific University. Joseph and Eve had been somewhat bewildered by the exposure and networking that had occurred. They would be returning to Djigouera with a book full of contacts and a huge amount of promised sponsorship. They were much encouraged — things had panned out far more spectacularly than they had imagined.

Benjamin contributed that his NGO, United Medical Aid had been able to attract considerable partnership interest, and its wide range of healthcare providers would enjoy significantly greater capacity. He was excited about the increased provision of mosquito nets into South Sudan. He had chosen his target country with great care as he knew that prying Western eyes would not gain access to this war–affected region for a considerable length of time. The truth was he had a clever little racket going. His supplier invoiced their sponsors for expensive highly effective nets while Benjamin shipped budget, low grade nets. These in turn were sold to the end user — admittedly at low prices, for a further return. Sponsors felt good about themselves, he turned a huge profit, the supplier also made a fortune and all the distributors had their piece of the pie too. Everybody gained handsomely out of the scheme except of course for those who received the mosquito nets and those who could not afford them.

Things had become a little sensitive since March 2014 when the UN Global Fund released damning data regarding corrupt sales of mosquito nets in Cambodia. There, one government official allegedly received 3.3% of the $12 million paid to two overseas suppliers of nets. That would be about right he had mused.

He could not risk discussion around this table about welfare delivery in Burkina Faso for example — not while those capable of assessing United's performance by commenting on the benefits being experienced by those in need were present.

The truth was Benjamin was as committed to the continuation of Africa's medical problems as he was to the elimination of them. His livelihood depended on a good stream of pictures and reports of helpless little African children needing a fat flow of US dollars to rescue them. Unless that flow continued and widened, Benjamin's ability to tap the pipeline for his own ends would be limited.

The food came and went, all of it wonderful. Eve stared in wonder at the presentation, the spotless surroundings, sparkling tableware. This dustless laboratory–like sterility was another world to her.

Seeing Laodicea

Despite Benjamin's best efforts to the contrary, talk turned to the predicament of farmers in the Burkina Faso / Mali border regions, where trader engineered famines and fickle weather conditions, made subsistence cropping a perilous existence.

Eve was a little shy with her English and overawed by the conversation of the men folk. Despite many years of exposure to European customs and some understanding of Americans, she was uneasy about sitting down for a meal with men and being an equal contributor to the conversation. However Casper, being genial and unstoppably persuasive and relational, managed to draw her out, discovering that she had grown up in a farming family with brothers who currently managed the family's land. He asked her what it was like to survive there.

Eve explained that survival was difficult and that most of her siblings and indeed her mother and other women of her compound had died young. She described the preventative health care that was almost non-existent. Medical intervention in problems that presented was expensive and almost useless. Having insufficient funds to access it had contributed directly to the death of many of her friends. It was at this point that Benjamin began to feel extremely uncomfortable. Whatever Casper had planned for this meeting was never going to happen now. He was too close to exposure to allow any further contact with these people. He just needed to survive the meal and get out of there.

Eve dropped the expected conversational grenade Benjamin was dreading by explaining how a doctor from an NGO named Light to Africa, had refused her step mother emergency treatment over lacking cash up front finance. She spoke factually and authoritatively as Casper drew out of her two critical pieces of information. First healthcare was routinely charged for at the point of need and second, Light to Africa was the only provider in her area.

The atmosphere around the table swiftly changed from light and affable to tense and heavy. Casper said quietly. 'Benjamin, didn't you say you once worked for Light to Africa in Burkina Faso?'

4

Benjamin laughed nervously, the pupils of his eyes narrowed, his breathing became shallow. He had been cruelly exposed. 'No you must be mistaken my friend. I knew of them and worked closely with them for a time, but was never employed by them. You must have misunderstood me.'

Casper was not an Ivy League top of class and successful entrepreneur by chance. He was a highly skilled negotiator, well used to verbal agreements and calling half-made statements into binding contractual agreements. He knew what he'd heard yesterday, and that Benjamin was lying now. He had some follow-up work to do on Dr Benjamin Traoré.

Casper changed the subject, seamlessly moving things along and relaxing the mood again. He wanted information relating to grain trading, something about which all those present were knowledgeable. His purpose in bringing the group together was to discuss how it might be possible to set in place a more just system of grain distribution, with external investment — one that was not subject to rigged markets which would lead to the unspeakable social blackmail weapon of death by famine for racketeering purposes.

They spoke at length of where trustworthy people could be found to create such a network. Again the dynamic of the group was devilishly complicated. Eve and Joseph were naturally cautious about naming their acquaintances. Treachery and misuse of political power were so endemic to their homeland that to do so could lead to their contacts being pressurised or threatened, even with death. What Casper was suggesting — the undermining and replacement of current trading structures would not come about without fierce opposition.

They were wise to be cautious.

Benjamin was listening carefully. Ostensibly a pillar of the Christian community with excellent governmental contacts, he would naturally be someone with whom such a conversation could produce forward momentum with the right people. In fact he was interested to know who might be the main players in this little

Seeing Laodicea

scheme. He had "friends" who would pay handsomely to be able to intervene early.

The meeting ended cordially with everyone committing to continue contact. Benjamin could not get out of there fast enough. He could never return to this table. The cloak of secrecy with which his heinous life was draped was paper thin to non-existent here. Too risky — run!

Later that night, alone in his sumptuous Four Seasons bed, Casper reviewed the day. He was pleased to finally be making progress in making the world a better place.

He had managed two minor victories this evening. The first was speaking to the hottest of women in the hotel bar, and not bringing her back here. Even as he thought about what could be happening right now he experienced a tightening in his lower abdomen as arousal kicked in. He smiled at himself; at least he still functioned, even if he was turning into some kind of a monk.

His second victory was that the television screen was blank, and his laptop was off. It was now two months since he had viewed even soft porn. He knew he was an addict and was prepared to admit it. Apparently that was a good start. He'd taken a little counseling and had been advised to avoid certain situations hence the small victories this evening.

Counseling had led on to attending a full blown 'Living Waters' programme lasting six months of weekly attendance. There he had addressed issues in his family, past relationships leading to all manner of unhelpful invisible ties, assumptions and commitments. He had come to realise that just avoiding unhelpful situations did not address the parts of his person that had needed healing. Having followed the programme through, he was living in the good of it. Some might look upon treatment of his addiction by addressing his brokenness as whacky. He had found it demonstrably helpful.

His mind turned to the very positive progress of the meeting earlier. Everyone seemed keen to explore a just and radical

6

response to the sinister trading arrangements operating among the poorest sub-Saharan families. He could not wait to get his boots on the ground and find out what could be done.

He was however convinced that there was something sinister behind the immaculate, intelligent, charming Benjamin. He would contact Light to Africa tomorrow and see if there was any information on him there.

Benjamin was awake late into the night, anxious. Lunch had unsettled him more than any meal for many years. That however was not the reason for his anxiety or insomnia. Sleep patterns for Benjamin were erratic. It was at night that his unconscious mind came out to play. He would begin the process of attempting sleep by focusing on things that comforted him. Sexual liaisons — he would imagine himself as some kind of *Lothario*, with delusions of grandeur, and fantasy acts of courage. He was the hero, the stud, the champion of his private world.

The problems came when sleep took him and his subconscious took over. Then the nightmares would begin. People pleading, faces filled with anger and disappointment, fear and distress filled his mind. He would awaken within a couple of hours, too tired now to direct his thoughts — forced in the darkness to entertain his fears and failings.

He became anxious about being anxious — about being sleepless. He slept eventually as always, fitfully and dreadfully fearful — the product he was told of cognitive dissonance. He was professionally committed to the wellbeing of the poor, and his psyche paid more than lip service to the values of the humanitarian organisations that currently and historically employed him.

He was also however fundamentally and criminally committed to himself. The yawning gap between the behaviour supportive of those two positions and the agony of living with his own actions was a form of torture in some ways worse than the dreadful deaths of the victims of his selfishness. Wherever his head went, his

Seeing Laodicea

memories came with him. Some days he just wished to blow his brains out in order to escape from his troubled mind.

Eve and Joseph slept in the relative luxury of their modest hotel, as they often did; unclothed. Having talked at length about the people they had met and the things they'd seen, given thanks to God for the wonders of the day and its implications for the girls and the orphans in their care; they lay first in each others arms and then spooned together; physically, spiritually, emotionally happy and at peace — married.

2. PINK

Candice Taylor adored pink, always had. She was a girlie girl despite her sporty streak. Always up for a challenge and fervently determined to achieve to the point of obsession, she still could not resist pink. It was a devastating combination when encountered by men, something Candice was learning could be a problem now that her focus was not running after a jock and making babies.

In terms of progress as a humanitarian, graduating from Pacific with a first–class Masters had in one sense been a breeze. Her aptitude for adaptation had been as natural as if she had been born for cross–cultural mission. Most of the course had been spent immersed in children's work among the slums of Phúc Xá ward in the Ba Mình district of Hà Nôi, Vietnam.

Here her love of children shone through as she learnt to treat minor injuries, remove hook worms with paraffin along with basic nutrition and hygiene. She dispensed loving care to the adorable street kids that daily attended the centre for schooling, sports and music coaching, feeding and bathing.

Seeing Laodicea

There in the slum Candice had found life in abundance among the rat poor, downtrodden victims of the terrible choices of choice–less parents; parents whose consolation came from bottles and needles — whose pointless existence was both enlivened and spoiled by gambling, fighting and prostitution.

Her little project breathed true life among the living dead. The kids had a chance to break free from the filth and the squalor by rising up with better values, adequate self–belief and education commensurate with better prospects. Squatting in the dirt, modestly dressed but stunningly proportioned and beautiful, she could not imagine a more fulfilling way of being, than to immerse herself in the half–light of this disease–infested, unappealing slum and illuminate it with the inner light God's Spirit had placed within her.

However, her position in Phúc Xá was an internship. The project was determinedly transferring to indigenous ownership thus could not find a place for Candice once her internship ended. Tearfully she had wrenched herself away from the finest months filled with the purest love her life had ever known.

And here, in Kottayam's Park Lane, Candice was admiring pink pearls. An American accent and dazzling smile had ensured she received the closest of attention of the shop keeper, and Candice's eyes sparkled with delight as string after string of perfect pearls passed before her eyes. She selected a gorgeous matching necklace and earring set and braced herself for the price.

'25 dollars madam, and we will gift wrap them for you.'

She could hardly believe it. Back in California, despite the fact that pearls were not particularly fashionable, a similar string would fetch $250 or even more.

Her mother's birthday present secured, she clutched the precious parcel to her chest and re–crossed the road to her hotel, glad of its air conditioned amenities, but aware that this level of luxury could not last.

She was here on a placement with Hungry to Whole International, a mission agency that had caught her attention. While assessing various ways to put her Masters training to the test and invest her life for the poor, Candice had stumbled across HWI.

HWI (pronounced 'why?' a neat little phonetic trick) had a three-phase approach to poverty. They began with the most basic of needs, the empty stomach and exposure to the elements. It was here that poverty always became most immediately noticeable. Without food, water and shelter, life ends quickly.

Phase one therefore, dealt with the immediate needs of starving bodies and getting people under cover.

Phase two looked at the medium–term goals of providing seed for next year's harvest, semi–permanent housing, tools and medicines.

Phase three — and here Candice had thrown in all her chips — was about the future. This began with microfinance for self-determined small enterprises; and stimulating them through professional input, into wealth generating businesses.

Income generation consequently helped tackle child mortality through preventative medicine, hygiene, and clean water wells.

Providing education for the next generation was vital. This, linked to business development training for high quality future products and effective routes to market, changed the aspirations of the community. These were the keys to finally ending chronic poverty.

Here in Kerala Candice would be joining an India–wide organisation committed to the poorest of the poor: the Church of the King of Kings (CKK).

From the hotel she was met by the driver of a Tata 4x4, who weaved his way maniacally through the insane traffic to a large and leafy compound where her induction was to begin.

Candice was not a racist. She had grown up in California, where racism — except towards Mexicans which was seen as OK — was

11

Seeing Laodicea

unusual. Its proponents were viewed as pariahs, social misfits; Duck Dynasty style cartoon characters not to be taken too seriously.

Candice had encountered no problems dating black men (she herself was a platinum blonde). In fact her most impactful love affair had been with the gorgeous, charismatic Casper Scales — easily the most wonderful man she'd met. Her thoughts drifted dreamily to Point Loma, shellfish at the Blue Wave and unhurried Sunday afternoons in Casper's perfect bay view apartment.

Her attention was snapped to the present by a British woman handing her an Overseas Visitor Guidance Pack that she was expected to ingest and follow. It would help her avoid the worst *faux pas* committed by foreign guests, apparently.

It did seem a little over the top since she had already been placed on location in Vietnam for two years and had gone through the HWI Stateside induction process prior to travelling here. But she was gracious about being talked down to. Rather that, than cause offence.

As she gave a tour of the campus her British host explained that a big part of the CKK compound was devoted to unconditionally loving Dalits.

Before the HWI induction Candice had never heard of a Dalit. If asked she would have suggested it was something Indian and edible.

She had however been informed in her training that Dalits were the lowest caste of Indian people dating back to the now defunct caste system affecting India before Gandhi — among others — ended it. Gandhi himself, though from a high merchant caste, had been subject to discrimination and violence while working as a lawyer for 21 years in South Africa. There the colour of his skin had been a problem to the ruling elite. He had from that time on, carried with him personal understanding of the rough end of discrimination and took a principled stance against it back in India.

12

Pink

Candice had been fairly bored during the seminar, and could barely remember what she'd been told. Here in a roasting classroom at the ministers' training facility on the CKK campus, things were brought into sharp relief. She wondered what a Dalit looked like. Her eyes roamed around the classroom, quickly lighting on a young Indian girl of around her age.

Prity Pasi was wearing a wonderful pink sari. Candice smiled as their eyes met. There was something irrepressible in Prity's eyes, something noble in her wide forehead. When Candice looked at her, taking in the gorgeous sari in her favourite colour, the lovely open face framed by glossy black hair swept into large loose plaits she knew that here was someone she could like.

Prity was slightly taken aback by the foreigner's level gaze. She had not expected to be noticed. All her life she had been accustomed to being overlooked or worse, mocked. Normally if an Indian visitor of high caste had looked upon her there would have been some level of sneer in their body language or voice — an institutionalised way of behaving of which perpetrators were generally unaware and victims almost instinctively just accepted.

For Prity was enjoying something Candice could not be expected to appreciate. Prity could discern that Candice was taking her at face value, appreciating her for what she saw: Prity in Pink.

13

Seeing Laodicea

3. UNCLEAN

Prity's journey to Kerala had begun in circumstances very different from Candice's. Candice came from a culture which had struggled through the civil rights movement, the steady progress of legislation and its enforcement leading to the emancipation of women. A land of equal opportunity irrespective of race, gender or creed was being shaped. Prity began life as a Dalit in India, perhaps the most oppressed, discriminated against and horrifically abused people group on earth.

Roshani Pasi was a lovely girl, born in 1983 to a family of manual scavengers from Becharaji, in the Mehsana district of Northern Gujarat. Her mother Vanita and father Jayantibhai both worked for a contractor to the Indian Railways, clearing excrement from a dry latrine by the local station. Her little sister, as yet just too young to work, attended the local Mehsani Gujarati language school. It was likely that next year at second grade she would have to stop her lessons because the family would no longer be able to afford the very modest school fees. She would at least be able to read, write and manage basic mathematics.

Seeing Laodicea

Roshani worked in the local matchstick factory. Here the work was backbreaking but she and her family saw it as a privilege to get work here rather than among the scavengers.

The work of the scavengers was utterly horrible and demoralising. Using only flimsy scoops, before dawn each morning they filled their baskets by scraping the latrines clear, lifted them onto their heads and carried the waste through the town to the designated dumping ground. No protective equipment had ever been issued to them by the employer.

On rainy days their task was made even more unpleasant as wet human waste would inevitably cascade all over them.

Both suffered from recurrent illnesses of the stomach and had difficulty eating because of the lingering stench their job necessarily gave them.

Both were bonded labourers, having inherited their task from their parents' debts. The process of bonded labour was a simple one. If underpaid Dalits fell into debt — almost inevitably — their children were taken into forced labour, and paid almost nothing. The innocent offspring usually repeated the cycle of bonded labour with their own children, as the pitiful income and the unjust trading regime in which they lived continued to drive them into debts of their own.

Interaction with townspeople of higher caste was almost impossible. The Dalits were considered unclean. They were not allowed in public places, could not enter restaurants — even if they could afford to — and were forced both to live and remain in the extreme east part of town, lest the prevailing wind blow their contamination onto members of higher castes. Even their dogs were prevented from socialising with dogs of higher castes, lest they should impregnate them; unthinkable.

Having finished her work for the day and run the gauntlet of abuse from the men at the crossroads where buses stop, Roshani made her way from their shack, to fill the family's water pot at the well, ready for overnight cooking and washing.

Dalit people were not allowed to use the town's main well for water; they had their own, older, shabbier Dalit facility. Roshani carefully worked the pump and steadily filled her container. While expertly transporting the pot home on her head, she cried out in pain as a sharp stone struck her thigh. A gruff male teenage voice attempting to convince the world that it had broken called out. 'Get back to your filthy hut you worthless harijan dog!'

Harijan was originally a term Gandhi had used to affirm the Dalits. It meant literally "children of the gods." However, such was the disposition of the higher castes to despise the Dalits that the meaning had been altered to infer "children of temple prostitutes," and had become a term of abuse.

Roshani knew that to reply would be disastrous for her, and she had to endure both the continued abuse of the young man and the sniggering of the girl he was out to impress while she hurried as carefully as her burden would allow out of range of his throws. He of course pursued her as far as he could be bothered, and she took two more stinging, cutting hits.

Roshani returned to the house fighting back tears. Vanita offered a comforting embrace and waited for her strong brave daughter to regain her composure. Self–pity and despair were bad options and both women knew it. Life was tough, and so were they.

Roshani went out once more onto the street, this time to buy a little flour and oil with which to make roti. Any purchases by Dalits in stores were conducted shamefully. The storekeeper would measure out what they asked for and throw it at them. If they dropped the purchase in the mud — well that was the consequence of being Dalit, not the responsibility of the thrower.

The little pantomime played out, as so many times before, with neither Roshani nor Ravi the store owner expressing any additional shame or disdain than was usual. Ravi despised the Dalit. It wasn't personal, it was cultural.

The Pasi family's employment, social and occupational predicaments should by now have been consigned to history. In

Seeing Laodicea

1993 a law was passed banning manual scavenging in India. Ever since Gandhi had brought his moralistic and peaceful approach to politics, passing laws and improving social justice had gained considerable momentum.

Progressive governments appealing to the electorate were "friends of the people." However, as it is in so much of the subcontinent, it's not in the passing of laws but in their implementation that there is a problem. From highway legislation to that banning child labour and trafficking for prostitution, there was one universal norm. Everyone ignored the laws, especially those relating to human rights; because those implementing and upholding them had a vested interest in the Hindu Caste system.

Those violated and in need of legal protection were very often the legal system's victims. Voiceless, friendless, unseen, untouchable and "backward," they had no redress in this world and no access to the deities believed to be beyond it. Abandoned by everyone and lower than cattle, the Dalits and "Other Backward Castes" with whom they were grouped endured hard lives in physical, emotional and mental anguish.

Perhaps it was some impetus given by the fresh wounds on her legs, or maybe the influence of a local newly arrived shopkeeper that triggered a series of events that would in one cataclysmic day change the future of the Pasi family.

Moses Christi was an extraordinary man. A handsome face adorned by a cheeky grin and rakish moustache topped by dark curly hair and athletic build, combined to give him an impressive, winning appearance.

With some difficulty, he had managed to secure accommodation away from the Eastern edge of town — despite being a Dalit. He was English educated and sharp-witted and some kind of external support allowed him to trade with suppliers and establish a novelty shop in which Dalits were able to make purchases on equal terms. In his shop they were treated with respect as customers. This in itself was a wonderful novelty, and

18

Moses and his lovely wife Rutu quickly built up a poor but enthusiastic clientele.

Unusually the shop was also frequented by those higher-caste individuals that were able to overcome their prejudice against a Dalit on account of the novelty products available at good prices along with the educated and charismatic nature of the store keeper.

Once established in his business, Moses Christi quietly began to talk to his fellow Dalits about the astounding choices available to them. He spoke of a mysterious three people God who welcomed all men, women and children, recognised no caste, identified with the downtrodden and promised justice.

All Untouchables were aware of the work done by the amazing Dr. B. R. Ambedkar, champion of the Dalit. Somehow he had risen from a lowly caste among the Dalit hierarchy to attain doctorates in political science, law and literature. Known as the Father of the Indian Constitution, he had worked hard — along with Gandhi — to try to abolish the social injustice suffered by the majority of Indians. He had pushed for the abandonment of the caste system, the root cause of the disease known as prejudice.

Untouchability was an embarrassment to Gandhi who as an international man of justice and human dignity admitted shame over the issue.

From 1947 Ambedkar had been appointed by India's high-caste rulers, who received power from the British, to chair the committee which drafted the Indian Constitution. In 1948 Gandhi was assassinated by radical Hindus for being 'too accommodating' — which gives some backdrop to the pressure both men were under at the time.

Ambedkar's constitution was adopted by the Indian parliament in 1949, though he objected to some clauses within the final document.

He went on to declare that he was born a Hindu but would not die one, and set about exploring alternatives.

He was much taken by the fact that Jesus Christ stood out against the caste system and Jesus' preaching challenged similar religious socio–spiritual bondage placed on people at the time of his ministry in Israel. However Ambedkar recognised that the church in India was complicit with the caste system and for that reason rejected it. So by 1956 he had chosen to become a Buddhist.

Ambedkar organised a mass conversion for Dalits in that year and although many did indeed convert to Buddhism, it was not the many millions he had envisaged — and subsequently did not bring down the caste structure as hoped.

The very fact that Ambedkar decided to challenge the Hindu caste system opened a way for many Dalits to understand that their spiritual exclusion and social bondage left them no way forward as Hindus. Seeking alternatives became fashionable, and left large tracts of India vulnerable to the aggressive politico–spiritual movements in the various forms of Islam. This was most visible in the creation of Pakistan where the spiritual (Islamic) and nationalistic partition of the sub–continent was negotiated.

Gandhi had found himself literally in the cross hairs of those who would not tolerate the continued cruelty of caste, and of those who knew that to release its prisoners would bring the working structure of Hinduism down. He was shot by Hindutva idealists; the radical Hindu thinkers that formed in response to the threat posed by alternative religions — particularly Islam.

So it was that a generation after all the excitement of reform and reconsideration of religion, Moses Christi gathered people to his home and spoke of freedom.

He explained that while the church had been rejected by Ambedkar, and rightly so, Jesus should not be so quickly dismissed. Moses belonged to a church movement that wanted

20

to more adequately represent Jesus by demonstrating unconditional love and total acceptance among Dalits.

The Pasi family had struggled to comprehend what this could mean for them. Acceptance, love, spiritual freedom to worship God; all of these things were closed doors. They had been told that the gods were offended if a Dalit attempted to worship them. Dalits were the most excluded of the excluded. Their socio-spiritual–economic prison was the perfect lockdown.

It was very difficult for the Pasis to process the reasons for hope when hope had been extinguished from their souls from birth. However, they believed Moses and began their own exodus towards a glimmer of hope in which they began to imagine that light could even exist in their lives.

Moses talked of the possibility of bringing a school to the community. It was 2001, and the leaders of his CKK church network had recently made a commitment to engage with the Dalit in a way which would set them truly free. CKK's initiatives included the provision of English schools — simply for the benefit of Dalits — as a demonstration of 'no strings attached' love. There would be no pressure to become Christian except the compelling persuasion of the obvious questions: 'What makes these people so wonderful?' and 'What is the source of their love?'

In time the Pasi family began to feel empowered and encouraged in their tough existence. They started to see that changes had taken place in the governance of the nation were not being experienced in their town. Things were not as they should be here.

It was during the day following the stoning incident, a scorching hot 19 May 2001 — that Roshani asked a question of her floor supervisor, Mr. Rajkumar Gadhvi. Gadhvi was a hard and decisive man, leading a team of harsh overseers, each of whom brutally ensured quotas were achieved.

Emboldened by the fact that hers was a matter of advocacy unrelated to this place of work, and trusting her employer to have

Seeing Laodicea

some understanding of legal rights, she had requested a moment of Mr. Gadhvi's time in which to ask his advice. Slightly flattered by the obvious awe in which she held his expertise, and moved by the comely figure and shockingly beautiful face of this ragamuffin Dalit, he had assented to hear her.

'My parents have been employed as manual scavengers since childhood, and are still repaying the debts of their parents. I understand that it is illegal to employ manual scavengers, and I wondered if there was any way they could be legally represented to have this matter reviewed?'

Her much rehearsed question came out rather awkwardly, the words unnaturally formal on her untutored lips.

In her naïvety, Roshani had stumbled upon the worst of advisors. A lifelong supporter of Rashtriya Swayamsevak Sangh (RSS), the military activist arm of the Hindutva radicals, Mr. Gadhvi's head reeled as he heard these heretical words. Though innocently and inexpertly spoken, they carried the power of injustice which must not on any account come into contact with just and legal representation. His eyes hardened but he spoke quietly enough. His words were measured, terrible and devoid of any humanity; the product of 3000 years of prejudice.

'You are wasting your time girl. What happens in Delhi happens in Delhi. Out here where their milk, oil and gas come from we do things differently. You have no right to be asking about such matters — you a dirty Dalit girl from a stinking shit–scraping family. Get back to your station and keep your delusive thoughts and questions to yourself.'

Roshani's little frame stiffened at the stinging words, the glimmer of hope she had wanted to pursue snuffed out before it could live. She returned, shoulders sagging, lip quivering, to her carriage of sacks of chemicals for the production line.

They came two nights later, silently at first and then with the splintering crash of a kicked in door. Swinging clubs thudded against the skulls and ribs of the sleeping family. Suddenly the night was rent with screams and sobs then pleadings then moans. Finally quiet again, except for the near imperceptible soft breaths of a tiny girl. The Hindutva–inspired RSS, merciless enforcers of the privileges and advantages held by the upper castes, had done to the Pasi family as they had done to Gandhi: silenced them.

They left behind the broken bodies of Roshani and Vanita, both gang raped and beaten to death. Jayantibhai died of a severe head trauma, and multiple organ rupture; the merciless result of uncounted blows all over his body from hammers and clubs. Theirs were three of 28,000 recorded acts of violence against Dalits in that year (four per hour), not including the 28% of Dalits denied access to police stations and thus unable to report anything.

They also left behind, tiny, silent and unnoticed among the bedding in a dark corner of the room and untouched except by terrible memories, Prity Pasi.

Just before dawn Prity called trembling at the house of Moses Christi. There was nowhere else for her to go. Warm chai and roti revived the traumatised child. Moses ran quickly to the house, gagged and immediately alerted the authorities who unhurriedly collected the bodies. No effort was made to identify the perpetrators; no charges were brought against anyone. A statement had been made among the Dalits; a good job done.

Prity needed to be moved. Rutu accompanied her by bus to Ahmedabad where the little girl and compassionate friend rested in a Church of North India (CNI) apartment. From there Prity was taken quietly to Palanpur up in the far north east of the state near to the Rajasthan border. Here she joined a CNI orphanage, donning a pink check uniform and disappearing among a mass of gap–toothed smiles and pig tails. She was soon enjoying the loving care of dedicated house parents under the supervision of highly talented church leaders.

And she got to wear her favourite colour.

Seeing Laodicea

4. UNITY

In Palanpur Prity was not a Dalit. Here she was just Prity Pasi, little girl. She had her duties as part of the strict regimen of the home, and she had English schooling paid for by the CNI. The CNI was among the more progressive Christian denominations, being in itself an amalgamation of multiple denominations which came together in 1970.

The little mission station which became Prity's home had planted three significant churches, launched an electrical engineering training centre, ran a health clinic to which visiting doctors and a permanent nurse were attached and was attempting to gain the necessary skills to start an IT training centre. All of this was for the benefit of the Mulnivasi. This grouping was a collective for those too low in the hierarchical caste system to qualify even for the jobs assigned to the Bahujans, the caste system's lowest rung.

The Mulnivasi in this region (which included the Dalit) were mainly those who had converted to Christianity, and these were plentiful. Viewed by the people around as outcastes, to have any chance of employment, they needed an edge; hence this training facility.

Seeing Laodicea

Working each day in the fields around the children's home, taking her turn in preparing food, washing the plates, metal spoons and metal cups, and serving from the large pots, all became part of a normalising structure for Prity's life. The well constructed and roomy two-storey home was largely self-sufficient in that it grew corn which became roti, chick peas, fresh vegetables and soft fruits. Labour was supplied by small willing hands, which quickly picked up the necessary skills to survive and thrive as part of a community of supervised children.

The climate was semi-arid, making subsistence farming very tough. The people of Palanpur were expert gardeners and farmers. Despite the lack of rain, irrigation was possible by the use of hand pumps and channels were dug to run precious water to the crops.

The aquifers from which water was drawn were kept as high as possible by the use of check dams. These were small mud built dams running across all the gullies on the local hills. Each dam prevented water from running off those hills and away in the rivers too quickly for the aquifers to fill. It was an ingenious and highly effective way of ensuring that the villages hereabouts had some of the finest and lush crop-producing land in the state.

For Prity, the cleanliness of the linen, the smell of the flowers and the cheerful chatter of happy children combined to make this a delightful place to recover. Slowly, week by week her resilience returned. The shattered, terrified grey-skinned scrap of humanity half carried here by Rutu began to be transformed into a beautiful relaxed and happy child.

Discipline was strict, and the ultimate sanction was a beating with a stick but such was the regime that this apparently was only usually applied to older boys from the home just along the road. The fact that corporal punishment existed and was a possibility deemed its actual use largely unnecessary. Behaviour was exemplary.

Avi, the church leader was in charge of matters of discipline and was a kind and gentle man. His was the drive behind the developments here at the mission station, and he was the church planter that had seen one congregation become three, each numbering between 200 and 500 congregants. He spoke seven languages and seven dialects (unwritten languages) enabling him to easily and personably engage with the locals. But his abilities were not restricted to linguistic skills; he played the drums beautifully, keyboard appreciably well and the guitar sufficiently well to lead worship gatherings. He had bachelors in history and masters in theology. A wonderful fellow, married to the hilarious and charismatic Rena. Together they offered excellent pastoral and leadership gifts to their scattered communities, in particular to the poor.

Sadly the activities of Hindutva-inspired activists were not confined to Becharaji, Prity's town of origin. They were militantly at work here in the hill country.

Avi received the news that a Catholic church had been burned in a nearby village. He met with Father Draved to console him and walk through the charred ruins of his premises. The two men embraced and committed to pray for one another. Avi carried with him a small financial gift — the most his churches could afford — to help with the restoration.

A few days later, evil tidings came from closer to home. Two families who were worshiping in the church led by his wife Rena, had been attacked. Everyone had been beaten and pelted with rocks but worse; one of the teenage girls had been raped by the hooded assailants. Her brother who had attempted to intervene had been stabbed to death. Avi's concerned and grim face peered in through the doorway of the darkened house of his suffering friends within minutes of being told. The hopelessness and despair among the family members was palpable. They would bury a promising young man, and stand with a violated and probably impregnated young woman — the next generation of their family ruined and despoiled.

Avi and Rena could find no words for the awful situation. Trite blessings and triumphalist prayers had no place here. 'Weep with those who weep' their Bible instructed.

Seeing Laodicea

There, on the neatly swept floor of the poor family's little home they beat the ground and wailed their dismay, tears splashing upon the polished concrete floor. Two smaller children, bewildered by what they had witnessed and frightened by the distress of the adults sat silently on the floor in the corner. Their huge eyes carefully watched in the lamp light, missing nothing.

Finally, after an extended time of empathetic grief, Rena arranged for food to be brought, though no-one felt like eating. But strength was needed. Then through the long first night of mourning the little family and its church leaders sat together quietly.

The local police made a desultory attempt to investigate the crimes. As was the norm, there was insufficient evidence to bring anyone before the courts.

Reports of more churches and Christian houses being burned came in over the subsequent weeks. The ruling Bharatiya Janata Party (BJP) was doing nothing to condemn acts of violence. In fact, since 1998, it had been insinuating that Christians were bringing such injurious attacks on themselves by forcibly converting Hindus. The authorities were slow to act in defense of the Christians and a sense of helplessness descended upon those who were wide open to what was clearly a targeted campaign to harass, harm and injure them.

Avi contacted Father Draved and the Alliance minister, Robinson Carpenter, also local to the area. All three had now experienced attacks on congregants and or buildings.

For the first time in any of their memories, Catholic and protestant believers knelt to pray together. They prayed for their communities, wracked by fear and cringing with a 'who's next' sense of foreboding. They prayed for the continued advance of the life-giving good news of Jesus Christ, impartial Prince of Peace, and for his influence to come and turn more hearts from anger and prejudice to compassion and embrace.

Finally they prayed for their attackers. They asked that God would pour out his forgiveness upon them as they suffered the torment of knowing their crimes would go unprosecuted and they would never be brought to justice. Thus with no chance of paying for their crimes their unassuaged guilt would likely haunt them to the grave. They asked God to grant them peace.

It was a Wednesday, the last Wednesday in September; but the first of many Wednesdays when this little group would meet before God and cry out for their people, and all those who felt threatened enough by them to act with violence.

By the end of October the spate of attacks had dried up. The Christians in the community held their breath. There was an angry and fearful sense of foreboding; something momentous was brewing.

On 13 November, Ganesh Halaji Desai, a prominent Hindu community leader asked to speak with Father Draved. He requested that the meeting should take place on land owned by the church. Draved, Robinson and Avi met together on Wednesday evening and agreed to get together with Mr. Halaji Desai on that Friday during daylight hours, in Rev Carpenter's church.

They chose this building because it had no orphanage on its land and thus eliminated the risk of violence to Christian children; a proviso that had ruled out Avi's property. Carpenter's place was still standing, which criterion had rather regrettably ruled out Father Draved's.

The time of the meeting was set for 2:00 pm and at 1:00 pm, fearing the worst, Avi kissed his children; carefully telling each how proud he was of them and looking them straight in the eye to express his delight in and love for each. The family prayed with thankfulness for all of God's blessings, especially for one another. Then Avi lingeringly kissed Rena goodbye, clenched his jaw, straightened his shoulders and drove round to Rev Carpenter's little church to face what the Hindus had in mind for him. The three leaders prayed briefly for courage, wisdom, love and

Seeing Laodicea

forgiveness to clothe them, and awaited the arrival of their adversaries silently, each alone with his thoughts. Rev Carpenter was especially grateful for the company of his fellow ministers. They could have left him to face this alone but had refused to do so.

Halaji Desai was precisely on time. He came apparently alone; at least there was no sign of anyone following him at this stage. The three ministers became slightly less tense.

The Hindu leader came quickly to the point.

'I have come to plead with you to call off your God,' he began.

'We have had enough. Please tell us what we must do to appease Him. Our gods are powerless to protect us against him and we need to hear your terms.'

Consternation swept the faces of the three Christians ministers. Avi was first to react.

'Mr. Halaji Desai, please explain your position. We are unaware of any hostility from our side. We are people of peace, seeking only the good of our neighbours.'

Desai looked agitated and wrung his hands, shifting in his seat. He appeared unwilling to explain himself but could see that to fail to do so might not secure the urgent settlement he sought.

'What I am about to tell you must remain between the four of us. If you quote me I will deny it; then it will be your word against mine with plenty of reason why you might collude against me, to undermine your evidence.'

The three church men listened intently.

'You may be unaware that the mobilisation of radical Hindu mobs against Christians in this region was orchestrated by three young activists. I am told that each has been personally involved in the attacks taking a lead role, as well as mustering many others for involvement in the violence.

In the last four weeks, the three men have each suffered terrible misfortune. One has been bitten by a King Cobra while working his land. He died within minutes. The second has been struck by madness and has been transferred to a secure unit in Ahmedabad where he has not responded to any treatment. It is feared that if he receives any more electrolysis he will be irrecoverably damaged. It would be better for him to be dead than as he is now. The third has manifested symptoms associated with Creutzfeldt–Jakob disease. He has been given less than one year to live.'

This information was received by the three ministers with genuine shock and horror. Nobody spoke; there was nothing appropriate to say. Desai continued carefully and quietly.

'It is our conclusion that your God has moved against us. Everyone that has followed these men is now living in fear. We are asking you to call him off. We appeal to you to do whatever you need to do to control him.'

Rev. Carpenter spoke.

'Sir you do not understand. Our God is not subject to the control of men, even if it is him that is moving against you. We believe he is the creator of all things including the spirits whom you worship. He is subject to no one and longs that all men would own his values and cease their constant misuse of power and the self-interested cruelty to one another.'

Desai nodded sagely and responded carefully.

'It is these lofty claims, and their power to influence the Backward Castes and Dalits, that have presented such a threat to the Brahmins and other privileged castes. It is for this reason that the Hindutva forces have specifically targeted Christians. Of all the alternative religions available to the OBCs and Dalits; Christianity is perceived to be the greatest threat.

'The expected exodus of millions to Buddhism precipitated by Ambedkar's treachery did not happen; mainly due to a lack of coordinated leadership among the Dalits. You Christians are more organised, and with the rising of the All India Christian Council it is possible that you will convince the Dalits that there is nothing for them in Hinduism.'

His shoulders sagged, defeated, his face a picture of anguish, personal fear and torn loyalties.

'It seems your God is fighting against us, even as you pursue the peace he demands of you.'

After a few moments of silent contemplation Avi felt it might be helpful to offer some advice.

'Throughout the pages of the bible we read, there are several examples of our God intervening in the affairs of social justice. This only happens when wickedness reaches a level in which his actions will have been found to be eternally just, proportionate and appropriate by his standards. It seems that it is possible to attract his attention by deeds so wicked that his desire for men and women to cooperate with their own understanding of right and wrong is outweighed by the urgency of responding to the needs of the helpless.

'It is possible that you have indeed offended God. If that is so then we cannot help you, for our prayers have always been for you, not against you.'

For the first time, real fear etched itself onto the face of Ganesh Halaji Desai. The majesty of the innocence of the Christians struck him like a blow. He knew his people were horribly in the wrong, and it seemed there was no solution but to face the wrath of a terrible untameable God.

Silence fell upon the little group. The large ornate clock on the wall of the study became the dominant sound in the room. Finally it was Father Draved that suggested a way forward.

'Perhaps if you were to hear our hurts, and were willing to confess your people's sins on their behalf, taking ownership of their actions, and truly undertaking to utterly change your behaviour our God would hear your humble heart and relent in his fierce anger. Our Bible says that, *"He will not turn away a contrite heart and a humble Spirit. It is his word; he is one who keeps his promises".'*

And so it was that those wounded from among the Christian community gathered in Father Dravid's church that Sunday, and one by one listed the horrors that had been visited upon them by the radical Hindus. Rena spoke for the two families who had been first attacked from her congregation. Neither family could bring themselves to describe the details of the suffering inflicted upon them. Their sobs as they heard Rena's words struck Desai like blows.

When eventually the last of those wounded or suffering losses from the attacks had spoken, Mr. Halaji Desai spoke on behalf of the Hindu leaders. He quietly and formally accepted the blame for the atrocities and attacks and damage listed, owning both the motives and the actions. He concluded with words of dignity and humility.

'Finally, I apologise to each and every one of you for what we have done. I solemnly give you my word that all such attacks will cease forthwith and will never be repeated. Furthermore, if you present to me a list of damaged property I will ensure that each is made good at the expense of the temple purse. Finally to the families that have suffered loss by death, violation or injury we will pay compensation.'

Avi responded on behalf of the Christians.

'We accept your apology and forgive you for what you have done. We release you from any guilt. Perhaps our God will have mercy on you; the matter is and always was between him and you.'

There was no improvement in the condition of the two activists still alive. However no further unexplained catastrophes occurred among the Hindu families in the ensuing weeks.

Seeing Laodicea

5.   KIDS

It was Rick, now heading up Pastoral Ministries at Ablaze church, who suggested that Casper should get in touch with the house building nonprofit that had so fired up Candice and precipitated his own epiphany. And so it was that on 1 April 2014 Casper pitched up at an address over at Precision Park Ave to meet the folks who'd indirectly busted up his life.

He wasn't sure what he was expecting, but what he got was a shock. Standing in a smart reception area fronting a converted factory unit, tapping his expensive Italian patent leather shoes on the hard wearing industrial carpet he looked at the exhibits on show. Various bits of memorabilia and branded clothing were displayed, and a book filled with pictures explaining the story of a bunch of radical humanitarians. It appeared this group had committed themselves to building houses for Mexican families who were trapped in terrible living conditions in the border areas.

Smack! He was hit squarely between the eyes by a ping–pong ball. Smack! Smack! Two more stung his cheek and ear respectively and he hit the deck behind a coffee table. A howl of triumph went up from the corridor as balls whistled and bonked

Seeing Laodicea

around him. Some crazy old fool with a pump–action ball gun had gone nuts. Instinct took over, and Casper went into game mode. Like lightning he was over the coffee table that had provided cover, down the corridor and bringing the psycho down with speed and style that would have made a Patriot's defensive tackle proud.

Woof! The air was forced out of Wild Bill Hickok's lungs.

'Oh shoot!' came a gasp. 'Y–you're not who I thought you were, are you?'

An old fella who appeared to be in his early 60s looked mortified as they regarded one another from a distance of two inches. The man was both pop–eyed and shocked, and once Casper rolled off his victim he was quickly overcome by paroxysms of mirth and aghast apology.

'Oh my, I'm so sorry! What can I say? ...I was expecting someone else — thought it'd be fun if I shook him up by coming out of my office like Rambo! Oh you're probably too young to know who I'm talking about, big guy, lots of guns and war and stuff; killed lots of people, never died.'

Blair had started to gabble. This was difficult as he was gasping breathlessly from a combination of exertion, embarrassed laughter and being winded.

'Impressive tackle, I must say' Blair gulped, giving Casper the raised eyebrow of respect. You should meet my boy! He's played a bit of football. So, who are you? Who have you come to see?'

'I'm Casper, just dropped by to see what you guys are about. You've been doing some stuff with my Church — Ablaze in Mission Valley. I was over this way and guess I wanted to check you out and inquire about getting involved in some way.'

'Uh, oh, wow I see. Well, help me up and we'll go through to my office, have some coffee and I can show you around. My name's Blair, I'm the CEO.'

Kids

It was quite an introduction Casper had to admit — rather more intimate than a handshake.

Casper was baffled. He instinctively liked this crazy dude, but what had happened was so far from his expectation of a humanitarian mission organisation that he didn't know where to begin collecting his thoughts.

He had prepared his opening lines, rehearsing in his mind an approach that would impress whoever came to hear them. Things had not exactly gone to plan.

There was one small consolation, Casper's baffled brain thought wryly; these people might be barking mad, but at least the gun only fired ping–pong balls rather than bird shot, it could have been worse!

A quick overview in Blair's office gave him a window on an incredible world. Blair briefly sketched out 34 years of pioneering appropriate humanitarian mission, of experimenting, and continually reviewing and upgrading ways of doing things. He spoke of renewing construction methods, supporting and advising connecting groups, and developing integrated ways of working with and empowering Mexican churches. Blair and his wife had spent their entire lives carrying a tremendous burden for the poor. The fruit of their work so far; an amazing team, thousands of friends, and 17,000 families appropriately housed. Wow.

'It's… well, I can't really explain it. We're just keen on trying to do what we think is right by the families, and God seems to open up opportunities for us to… Oh wait, is that the new iPhone 5S? Man I gotta get me one of them as soon as the 6 comes out and the price drops. 64–bit, what does that mean anyways? Does it have the image stabilising thing and the upgraded camera, or is that the 6?'

The topic of conversation had abruptly changed. Before he knew it Casper was outside admiring Blair's home–built suction pads and string Go Pro setup for the Rav4 in the car park.

Seeing Laodicea

'Set it to take a shot every ten seconds then I can just drive through the communities and among the teams without anyone really noticing they are on camera. Kinda tells it like it is much better than all those posed shots the groups post up on Facebook. They're good and all, really useful for people to get a view on what happens across the border but I don't think you can beat a candid shot.'

Then he was off on some other track, talking about how he was always trying to look at ways to use emerging technology to help them in their work.

'I often seem to find myself in Fry's looking at stuff and dreaming. Wanna get me one of those Skycams next. I need to know what kinda noise they make when they're flying though. It'd be real neat to take candid shots from the air but I'm thinking everyone would be looking up at the drone all the time. Could turn into a distraction and I don't want that.'

Casper smiled and just stopped himself from breaching the Espionage Act 1917 and 18.USC.798, its more recent amendment. He had the perfect tool for this old timer. One arm of Droneview Inc. in which Casper still held considerable shares had been working on a military–grade front line hand–launched surveillance drone with whisper engine technology, munitions resistant airframe, and equipped with infra red, low light and high resolution camera technology. That would get Blair his candid shots OK — although a bit beyond his budget — and certainly off limits for this conversation!

'You know I do a live radio show in South Africa once a week from pretty much, anywhere I'm travelling at the time. Just rig up my gizmos and away I go. Even four or five years ago it just wouldn't have been possible. Amazing how times change.'

The conversation had changed track again. Casper's focus intensified still further. Africa! He knew about these guys and Mexico but was not convinced — whatever Rick said — that he wanted to be grubbing around in Mexico. Africa was closer to his heart.

Casper reviewed the last hour of his life. In that time, he'd been shot at with an impressive pump–action toy gun, he'd brought down a nonprofit CEO with a fine cover tackle, enjoyed a mini tour and potted history of an incredible humanitarian outfit and found himself looking for military–grade solutions for holiday snaps.

He instinctively liked Blair even if he found it hard to keep up with the sudden dramatic rerouting of conversations. Here was a man at ease in his own skin. He wasn't doing anything he didn't want to do, wasn't denying the person he was born to be, nor was he shirking challenges. He was natural, affable, and fun. When Blair moved through the building, nobody stiffened at the approach of the boss. There was high–five action and back–slapping all round.

Comparisons with Casper's tight–lipped professional world were inevitable. Everyone in his outfit looked immaculate, presented flawlessly, worked intensely. Even Chuck, his seemingly irrepressible playboy best friend, had been tamed by the pressure of fronting high–value sales pitches. Possibly Marcus, the engineering genius driving the technological development side of CaMPuS Solutions, was the nearest of his two closest friends to staying normal. Casper smiled handsomely — normal for Marcus was nuts anyway. He was turning into Doc from *Back to the Future*; wonderfully weird, dangerously wired.

As he drove away from his encounter with Blair, Casper glanced down at his scuffed $400 shoe and the creased pants of his designer Armani suit. He resolved right there in his Porsche to do three things immediately.

First he would send Blair a healthy donation for water filtration equipment, school bags and blankets for the families. Second he would arrange for a Skycam pro 2 personal drone with iPhone control pack to be delivered to the nonprofit for his attention. He'd also get his assistant to slip in a realistic rubber spider to give the old boy a shock when he opened the package.

And finally, Casper would travel to South Africa with Blair in July. He was carrying a huge amount of guilt about the damage his

Seeing Laodicea

trading had done in Africa and was keen to go there alongside someone he could trust and do some good.

And so it was that thee months later, Casper was making his way through the arrivals hall of Johannesburg Airport, accompanying a delightful family from Tennessee and looking to rendezvous with a team from England *en route* to the township of Botleng near the mining town of Delmas up in the hills to the East.

The English party was all rigged out in matching blue hooded sweatshirts and thus they were not hard to find in the crowded terminal. Sarah from the nonprofit gave him a cheery wave and introduced him to Richard, a little English fellow whose friends called him Dick. Richard seemed pleased to see him, in a weary, jet–lagged way. Casper's first thought on meeting him was 'Why don't they fix their teeth?'

A large chap, who seemed to know his way around led them out to two dilapidated old coaches. 'You cannot be serious' thought Casper, who hadn't seen such ramshackle vehicles for some time — let alone thought about getting in one.

Apparently they were serious, and Casper was soon wedged next to some hairless rugby–playing creature from London who seemed determined to crowd him off the edge of his aisle seat and onto the floor.

Sitting among a coach–load of British teenagers was an odd experience. Their language was surprisingly profane and the topics of conversation ranged from the FIFA World Cup, in which Casper had a passing interest, through various celebrities, none of whom Casper had heard of, to sexual exploits on the beach. For a sex addict, this was unhelpful, especially as the main contributor to the conversation was a not–unattractive teenage girl.

The little party stopped off at a lion park where they were fed sausages, which were tasty and good and some sort of mashed starch with a texture like cotton wool that was tastelessly unpleasant. After a drive through lion pens in a caged truck, Casper was invited to pet the lion cubs. This he declined on two grounds: first, cats invariably bit him; second, these cubs had clearly been rolling in urine.

In the gift shop he bought an over–sized carved giraffe. He was not sure why, and only on his return to the coach did he begin to consider how he might get it on a flight home.

Finally after a diverting if not somewhat tortuous sightseeing day, the party arrived at some kind of a hostel. Here he was shown to a room which he was expected to share with three other men, each a youth leader. The bunks in the room were approximately 12 inches apart. Casper didn't fancy waking up and finding himself breathing across a narrow gap into the snoring face of a strange Englishman.

Casper and another fellow hunted down alternative beds in the main walkway between two accommodation blocks. It would have to do. At least the bed was slightly wider than the bunks, which suited his large athletic frame.

The British party was here to build two houses in Botleng. All the materials and the production of the foundation slab on which the houses would be built had been paid for by their trip fees. He was very taken with the overall concept and excited to be part of something life–changing for a family in need.

His first significant error came to light when it was time to turn in. He had not properly read through the briefing pack provided pre–trip, and had consequently packed for Africa — a hot country obviously. But it was extremely cold here. Apparently, winter in South Africa exactly corresponds to summer in the Northern Hemisphere.

The queuing system for showers hadn't been explained to him, and not confident of where he might fit into it, he showered last. Thus the water was freezing. Now stripped down to his designer boxers, his knees began to tremble with cold.

The beds were equipped with two blankets and one sheet each, which the cold penetrated mercilessly. It was not long before his shivering frame drove him to his voluminous grip bag. He slipped on two teeshirts, a tracksuit and some sports socks, falling asleep eventually.

When Casper awoke his feet were like blocks of ice and the air around his mouth turning to clouds of condensation with his breath. It was not until the sun had risen to high in the sky that he began to feel warm again.

Today there was more sightseeing to be done, this time in Soweto, a township made notorious during the ANC's struggle for the end of apartheid.

They visited the Hector Pieterson museum where for the first time Casper became aware of some of the complexities involved in South African racial conflict.

Hector was just 13 years old in 1976 when he died suddenly on 16 June. He was shot in the head by South African security forces while on a march with between 10,000 and 20,000 people led by primary school children. They were protesting at being forced to take their lessons in Afrikaans. A line of trees runs from the place where he was shot to the doors of the museum. Hector became posthumously famous because he was photographed while being carried from the scene, his distraught sister by his side.

Casper stood in front of this image, reproduced in huge scale outside the main doors of the museum.

The head trauma, clearly visible in the photograph, emphasised to him the awful reality of what had happened to Hector.

Inside the museum he learned that the death toll that day was 176, though the truth and reconciliation hearings subsequently revealed the ability of the security forces to completely destroy bodies. The likely figure was significantly closer to 700.

Kids! Children! Shot down! The world had recoiled in horror, and from 16 June 1976 onwards apartheid was mortally wounded.

One piece of learning particularly stayed with Casper as he shivered in his corridor bed that night. A museum exhibit consisting of three school desks told the little known story of the amazing primary school teachers working in the church supported mission schools operating in Soweto in the 1960s and 1970s. He was inspired to have read that they held extra classes at 06:00 hours to ensure that their kids scored 'A's and 'B's rather than simply passes. They believed in these little children and set them up for futures of hope. Nobody remembers these teachers, nor the 175 to 700 little corpses whose names were not Hector Pieterson, but a nation was changed and that was a fact.

The following morning Monday 14 July the team travelled out into the middle of Botleng Township for the first time. Here they drove through row after row of corrugated iron huts housing thousands of families. Each hut was unique, and yet each was the same. Grinding poverty laid out in a grim tableau as far as the eye could see. There was evidence of new builds taking place, in fact 20 or so foundation slabs were being constructed. The building materials for modest brick–built homes were laid out beside them, and enthusiastic bands of workers toiled to advance the construction. This was the government's scheme to house people.

Casper enquired about how the houses could be accessed. 'Become an ANC activist or wait 25 years,' was the candid response from a youth group leader; himself a white lifelong ANC party member, based in the UK. What began as a just political movement with lofty ideals was steadily moving towards a majority–protecting special interest group. Years of splintering, violence, struggle and coping with holding power had eroded the moral stance of the giants who founded the party. Already the ANC was calling the populace to give it the black vote. Mandela would never have allowed such talk. For him a vote had no colour and neither did a ruling party.

The first thing that Casper noticed when he alighted from the coach was that there were very many houses in this particular concrete road that were properly built. Between them there were corrugated iron shacks, but it seemed a decent part of town.

Seeing Laodicea

Richard explained; 'Just a couple of years ago this was all corrugated iron. We built those two, and that one and other teams built those. These other better dwellings have been put up in the last three years. This street is transforming. It is unrecognisable from how it was.'

Casper was visibly impressed, seeing with new eyes the progress that the teams had brought.

Very quickly the young people went to work snipping and sawing panels of rigid wire–framed expanded polystyrene, and wiring them together. In a single day they had formed and erected two three–room houses with double–pitched roofs. Not one of the team had a day's professional building skill, though three had built a similar house on expeditions like this, previously.

The second strikingly noticeable feature of the township was the children. They were everywhere, happy, laughing, wanting to be picked up and swung around. Casper did reps with two on each arm, much to the delight of his team. Little shows of athletic excellence were helping him fit in.

Late in the afternoon, he noticed a game start up where the local children started hurling themselves at the pile of sand that was required for the stucco, which eventually would complete the main body of the house. He nipped smartly out to halt the game holding out his arms like some enormous landing goose as he headed them off. What had been a mild diversion now turned into a main event, with children arriving from all angles. Casper tried desperately to head them off, but he had created a wonderful game — get past Casper!

He became more and more frustrated as the neat sand pile was spread rapidly into an amorphous lump, and shouted to bring order. A couple more team members came over, and finally the kids began to calm down. Then, sullen over the spoilsport behaviour of Casper the kill–joy, some of the older boys mimed using flick knives on him. Looking him straight in the eyes the children made imaginary stabs at his stomach and mimed slitting him wide open all the way up, laughing scornfully in his face.

44

Casper was shocked and horrified to see such malevolence surface among such carefree happy kids. Here was a community poised to go either way. Their future hung in the balance and so much depended on how parents, schools and community leaders influenced this generation to ensure that it chose not to opt for violent solutions.

He shook his head as he turned to clearing up the sand heap — kids!

They all returned to the hostel tired, happy, fulfilled.

Each evening a local pastor came and addressed the mainly English team, over dinner. One recurring message came through as successive speakers explained something of their story.

'I was brought up to hate the blacks. It was all we ever knew. We hated them.'

'When two whites beat my father within an inch of his life I grew a hatred for them that burned in me.'

'It was the culture to despise them. My parents' generation just expected us to continue the fight.'

'I never thought the day would come when I could forgive them. It just wasn't in my mind to think that way.'

Racial hatred was culturally new to Casper. He knew all about the civil rights stuff in the 60s in the US but he was a child of the late 80s, a generation later, under a black president. Of course there was prejudice and tension in his own city, especially when the police did something unnecessarily brutal to a black kid. Maybe for him tribalism was more acceptably expressed towards Mexicans and Moslems than black Christian Americans. In the college football subculture in which he had been immersed, throwaway lines like 'on our team even the white boys could fight' revealed a deep respect for the physiological advantages of African origins. Genuine systemic colour prejudice was another world to him.

Seeing Laodicea

Here in South Africa, the hatred was current, and the changes, brought about by Mandela's government were still working through. These guys were still processing their own journeys of forgiveness. Sometimes the language they used and the way in which they spoke of those from across the racial divide betrayed a journey that had considerable distance untraveled.

Despite the cold, bone weariness ensured that Casper slept, and dreamt of kids; some with flick knives.

6.   FREE RADICALS

Candice enjoyed Kerala. She found it beautiful, leafy; lush. She discovered that she was in India at a fascinating moment in its history.

Andra Pradesh had been divided into two separate states on 2 June 2014 — a few days before she arrived — converting India into a 29-state country. The former capital Hyderabad had now become capital of the newly recognised Telengana and thus Secunderabad, separated from Hyderabad by a sizeable lake, had found itself in a new state where the driving forces in the changes were to be found in Muslim dominated neighbouring Hyderabad.

The more Christian Secunderabad was apparently uneasy both about this change, and with the appointment of President Narendra Modi. People were politically unsettled and nervous. Modi, a former prominent RSS member, was known for his history of embracing Hindutva ideology. The Christians, even down in Kerala far to the South, were expecting a steady stream of minority-repressing legislation as his office became established. They were bracing themselves.

Seeing Laodicea

In spite of the worries relating to the seismic political backdrop, life in Kerala was proceeding as normal. Candice was absolutely stunned by the campus and the amazing impact its work was having in the nation.

She had been shown the pastor training facility, and had heard of the dream to make it possible for 25 million Dalits to be worshiping in well–led churches by 2025. They had already planted more than 3000 churches, and were looking for 22,000 more through a process of exponential multiplication growth.

She had seen the advocacy centre where lawyers worked on cases on behalf of Scheduled Castes and OBCs who had suffered violations and could not get justice.

She had been impressed by the school and the shrine prostitute rehabilitation facility, where there was training for employment and counselling available to those abused by the temple system.

Furthermore, the clinic, and hospital under construction were impressive. They were wonderful evidence of a deliberate approach to bring preventative medicine as well as medical intervention to those currently without the means to afford it.

All of the above was specifically set up to demonstrate the unconditional love of God to the Dalits. The motive was of course blended with a desire to see them come into relationship with the living God. However the leaders were implacably determined to hold to an unconditional love principle as a demonstration of the veracity of their message.

'So, um, this is how you see church?' She asked the question of her British guide, the only non–Indian national she'd met.

'Well of course we do, what else did you think Jesus asked people to do?'

Candice thought back to Ablaze with its fabric committee and missions planning board, worship team and bible study groups. 'Nope, nothing there he specifically asked us to do' she mused.

'So how long have you been working with the Dalits?'

'Ten years.'

'What! You've come this far in ten years?' Again Candice's mind flew back across the oceans to Ablaze. In ten years they'd planted one extremely wealthy, largely self-interested, not very big congregation.

As she made her way across the compound to meet the Bishop, Candice was deep in thought. She had just been exposed to what radical Christianity looks like. It was not radical in the way that fundamentalist sects of all creeds normally manifest themselves — violent attrition. It was a place of radical love.

So if radicalism is the product of the distilled essence of what a movement is about, when hatred is its expression, the heart of the movement is revealed as hatred.

'What a test of a community's creedal principles that was!' she thought.

'If democratic freedom is most radically expressed by dropping bombs on those who present a challenge to its self-interest — and conversely suicide bombs most radically express the desire to impose submission on those of non or different Islamic adherence then each exposes a callous heart!'

Still deep in thought, Candice slipped off her shoes and sat in a curious circular office apparently built above a water tank. This place benefitted from air conditioning, altering the air temperature down from 45 degrees (113F back home) to a heavenly 22 degrees.

A tiny man of South Asian appearance (who could have been from Hong Kong to Candice's eye) greeted her. He explained that he originated in the North East of India, the State of Manipur, which bordered Myanmar. Candice began to appreciate the amazing blend of peoples that made up India's population as

Seeing Laodicea

she realised this man's physical appearance was more akin to Chinese than Indian.

The Bishop wore a purple shirt, and a wooden cross. Apart from these props, he was indistinguishable from those around him, neither more nor less smartly dressed, his manner and demeanour similar. He was very pleased to meet her, taking a great interest in her background. Candice found herself telling him about what a flying cheerleader does, how American football works, and what she had been doing in the slum in Vietnam.

He countered with some information about Katching, his home town near Imphal, and how life there had been something of a struggle for his people particularly since the uprising.

The Bishop went on to speak with each of the visitors including a girl called Prity, with whom he became visibly even more tender and compassionate. He was a gentle man and seemed to have plenty of time. Each person to whom he spoke was made to feel unique, valued.

If she had been honest, before meeting this lovely fellow, she might have been tempted to imagine some degree of pomposity. The title Bishop seemed to suggest pomp, show; maybe the trappings of religion rather than anything tangibly good.

She came away with the distinct impression of having been given a small foretaste of what it might be like to meet Jesus. It gave her considerable comfort to know that underpinning the leadership of this fast-growing movement stood a man like this. Gentle, loving, generous in his manner; this fellow had been willing to show care and attention to strangers, and it seemed to come naturally to him. She wondered what suffering lay in his past that had made him so patient. Something about this little Dalit leader hinted at trials passed, tests he had overcome.

Owing to the changes brought about by the new government, Candice was not allowed to stay on Campus overnight, but was transferred to her hotel in Park Lane. There she resolved to commit herself to radicalisation. She had established a first principle on which she could make sense of all her actions. 'Live a life of love.' Commitment to radical love was the appropriate course of action for someone set free of this world's tawdry power struggles.

She slept the sleep of the just, dreaming dreams of bringing hope to the hopeless.

The following day, having been given a clear understanding of the expectations of Hunger to Wholeness International, Candice enjoyed a conference for team leaders from all around India. The conference was chaired by the two Bishops present, and was an opportunity for the team leaders to each explain what was happening in their State, to tell of good things for mutual encouragement and present challenges for prayer.

The keynote speaker, J. D'Souza explained the ongoing struggle for the emancipation of the Dalits. He urged all those present to continue in their efforts to love the underprivileged. He declared that a message pertaining to be good news to the poor but which did not contain any substantial change for the poor was devoid of authenticity.

Here was a man, thought Candice, who would not back down in the face of adversity. A lion in sheep's clothing, like so many of these radical lovers of the poor. She feared for their safety. They did not.

The main language used was of course English, as all the states represented spoke different languages and dialects. All of the leaders were English educated. This arrangement was especially convenient for a US participant. She was however somewhat thrown by the idioms and vocabulary at times, which were derived from England and not the USA. Thus trunk became boot (confusing when asked to stow luggage), sidewalks became pavements, and pants seemed to cause consternation whenever she referred to them.

Seeing Laodicea

Candice particularly enjoyed the breaks in the programme where she was free to circulate among the leaders and listen to their conversations.

She was drawn to a little knot of people from Gujarat state. It was to the town of Palanpur in Gujarat that she would eventually be posted. Her posting was apparently the reason for the girl Prity's presence here at the conference. They would be working together. A team leader by the name of Ramu was explaining some recent outreach work among a particular family in Palanpur, consequently Candice became extremely focused as she listened.

'As we worshipped God she began to make a strange ululating sound and lifted her hands above her head, bending the wrists so her they flapped loosely inwards and waving them so rapidly that they were just a blur. This happened every time we sang. When she responded to ask for prayer for her disabled son and we began to pray, it happened again. It was as though she was oblivious that she was doing it.'

'We have seen something similar with one of our women, and another sometimes slithers around on the floor like a snake when we come to worship God.'

'It is as if the spirits surface to contest ownership of the person in the presence of the Spirit of God.'

'Brothers we need to pray and fast to gain mastery of our own selves in order to drive these spiritually oppressive things from our people. Only when they are set free can they fully choose to worship the living God.' This from an older man named Mojis.

Candice was a little unnerved by all this talk of spirits. She was among Asians, so she was expecting some of this kind of primitive tribal stuff. However as she compared the progress Ablaze had made in ten years to what these guys had achieved, she was forced to wonder if what she represented could hold a candle to what was happening here. What was it she had learned from that Coloradan fellow on her first mission trip down to Mexico? 'We

52

come to learn, we come in humility. We do not assume that the way we do things is right — only different.'

She resolved to talk with Mojis when she got the chance. That opportunity came up quicker than expected as she found herself in a small group with him and Prity. The session leader had asked everyone to get into groups of three and prepare a timeline detailing their journey through life to date.

'Oh great,' thought Candice. 'This is where I get to write down my list of personal catastrophes so everyone can pick through my laundry!' She scribbled on her page the high and low points of her life–journey along a line bisecting the page horizontally with time marked off in years running left to right. 'Let me see now,' she thought and carefully annotated her dots;

- Cheerleading success and limited fame.
- Parents break up.
- Place at SDSU.
- String of boyfriends as I look for comfort. through sexual power, each time cheapening my own self–worth.
- Encounter God in Mexico and feeling rubbish about where I am at, getting a determination to change.
- Break up with the most amazing man I've ever known when he gets intimidated by my ethical challenges, freaks out and dumps me.
- Discipleship struggles with Pamela and Rick.
- Waitressing at a run–down Thai restaurant.
- Selling up anything of value.
- Masters degree in mission.
- Appointed to a minor role in a tiny not famous project among street kids in Vietnam.
- Hired by HWI.

It was hardly a glorious list.

Seeing Laodicea

When it came time to explaining their time–lines and the stories that lay behind them, Candice listened tearfully to Prity's story. Suddenly her own tale of woe interjected with moments of spiritual awakening and triumph paled into insignificance as this heroic young Dalit woman offhandedly outlined her story. Prity explained what it was like to first overcome the trauma of having her family devastated, then adjust to life in an orphanage. She went on to achieve top grades in all subjects completing high school before travelling to the state capital Ahmedabad to gain a first–class Bachelor's degree in Social Science at B. D. Arts College for Women.

She had taken some minor modules in economics and was interested in the link between economic development and political influence.

Having taken up a discipleship programme with the movement based here in Kerala, living in their Ahmedabad base, Prity had impressed the local leadership with her intellect and drive. She was the obvious candidate to work alongside Candice in the development of startup businesses primarily for Dalit women in Gujarat state and was highly excited about her new role in the partnership with HWI.

Mojis explained his key points slowly and without bitterness. He had, through excellent academic prowess gained scholarships to progress beyond his Dalit Education Centre school grades. He eventually entered one of the associate colleges of a leading Gujarati University.

At every stage in his schooling he had been mercilessly bullied and had gone on to be constantly reminded at university that he had no right to be in higher education. One of his lowest points had been hospitalisation with broken limbs having been thrown from a first floor window as a prank by "boisterous" upper–caste lads in his first semester. Nobody had been disciplined; it was his word against everyone else. Everybody had an alibi.

A high point for Mojis had been the undertaking of a 40–day fast. It was during this time that he mastered his thought life, focused on his temptations, and walked out on them. He explained how from that point on he had become free from compromise in terms of what his goals were. He had noticed since then that when he came to confront evil spirits they had been anxious to leave their victims at his command.

Candice saw her chance to bring a genuine enquiry — airily enough phrased — but behind it lay a worldview challenge. She, being as complex as the next woman or man was not able to isolate a pure motive from a hidden agenda of challenging self-assertiveness. Yes, she was inquisitive, but she was also keen to reaffirm her own opinion of how the world works.

'You mention evil spirits quite a lot. Why are they so prevalent in your ministry and so important to you?'

It was Mojis' turn to look bewildered. The response was too obvious to need an explanation and he didn't want to patronise this lovely young American with the enquiring level gaze.

'Many people here have spent their whole lives worshipping and communing with evil spirits. They know them by name, make offerings to them, and celebrate their birthdays. They become spiritually joined with them and take and renew all kinds of ceremonial vows pledging covenanted relationship with them.

For these people, knowing Christ is nearly always preceded by a power encounter between the Living God and the gods of their life until the point at which they choose to relate to him. It is not an issue of convincing minds; for them the benefits of worshiping the Living God are obvious when they are released from the grip of their demons. Without the ability to discern and remove demons, we would not make much progress among the Hindu peoples.'

'So that was clear then' thought Candice. 'He really did believe in all this stuff. '

Mojis wasn't finished.

55

Seeing Laodicea

'We have seen remarkable healings as people have been set free. We've seen deaf ears opened, crippled joints freed and lame limbs walk. We have seen those with scrambled minds and chronic depression wonderfully released and returned to peace. It is so much more than a matter of beliefs in the mind; the whole person is affected by spiritual malaise when evil spirits are worshipped.'

'I need to see it,' thought Candice, joining the ranks of many followers of Jesus, including one of the original twelve, for whom the ways of the Kingdom were so far beyond their experience that their personal spiritual authenticity gyro was overwhelmed. Imperceptibly she had shifted in her understanding but was not ready to capitulate to Mojis' spiritual worldview without some hard evidence.

Finally, it was time for Candice to share her journey. She was quite used to doing this, and was relaxed about being honest and open about her brokenness. Early in her account she observed Mojis becoming visibly uncomfortable. He excused himself, and she continued with just Prity.

It was many months before she realised that to openly raise accounts of sexual practice in Indian Christian culture at all was to attempt to cross a social electric fence. To do so in mixed company was a social disaster akin to publicly soiling oneself.

7. KEYS

If Casper saw one more hawk full of stucco he would most likely bury his face in it. For four entire days he had mixed, barrowed, scraped, smoothed and finally buffed stucco, a cement based mortar. They plastered on two coats, inside and out, to a 21' x 21' single–storey house with maddeningly extensive interior walls stretching up to the apex of the pitched roof.

The little team around him was incredible. This was a group of approximately 30 kids, none of whom had any construction experience. They worked hard through the heat of the day, picking up skills quickly and clearly enjoying getting plastered in stucco while experiencing something rather wonderful. Before their eyes and under their hands a house was forming for Ibrahim.

Ibrahim and his brothers had been living in the corrugated shack at the back of the property for many years since their parents moved to the area. Sadly both parents had died, leaving the brothers to fend for themselves from their mid–teens. Ibrahim was in his early 20s now and earning a little money. His surviving two brothers were both away in the city this week, earning money in

57

Seeing Laodicea

temporary jobs. They would return to find absolute transformation at their address.

Somehow, doing manual work and joining in the inevitable banter that shot between the little groups of British teenagers who came from various towns across the UK, made Casper's stress-laden weariness begin to fall away. Their diverse accents amused him too. With the functional parts of his brain and his body engrossed in laborious — and actually quite physically demanding toil, his mind was free to roam.

With advice from Rick and Pamela back at Mission Valley, he had begun to ruthlessly prune back his work schedule. At first this had been difficult. His was a psyche driven by success. The part of his brain which released the reward chemicals kicked off spectacularly when it didn't get what it demanded. He'd given it something of a hard time lately, what with total sexual and gambling abstinence, and mostly success in avoiding porn.

His reward sensors registered clamorous outrage, almost unbearable demands, and finally simmering resentment. He was teetering on the brink of depression. Starving himself of what he'd previously gorged on wasn't a spiritual detox; it was mental torture. A gravitational pull towards the yawning black hole in his life, of indulgence, had been inexorably drawing him back towards his former ways. He knew it was only a matter of time before he was going to allow himself to be the victim of an 'unforeseeable' and unfortunate slip–up.

Accountability to caring friends was all very well as an aspirational choice, but it was becoming an asphyxiating constriction to lifestyle choices. Choices that were so naturally appealing it seemed wrong to deny them. Here on the work site his tired mind began to fantasise, excusing itself on grounds of self–pity; travelling along familiar well–worn paths of hedonism.

Casper felt a dampness in his crotch and puzzled, reached down to investigate, discovering that one of his fellow group leaders had thoughtfully and sneakily filled the front pocket of his rather trendy baggy jeans with stucco. There was sniggering around the room as he painstakingly emptied it. Any one of three culprits, he decided. Oh well, he'd have to prank them all! Casper hadn't been treated so contemptuously in a long while. Everyone he knew fawned all over him back home. They all wanted a piece of him; he was either leading his team to another business development landmark making investors a fortune, or getting boffins' ideas to market. Such performance and a driven, uncompromising demeanour had made him relatively unapproachable.

These clowns from across the pond hadn't a clue how powerful and famous he was! He loved the anonymity; it was refreshing to be the butt of jokes, rolled in mud, treated like a brother. He could take care of himself in the rough and tumble, and his easy good humour naturally warmed to these guys. It wouldn't help them escape his revenge back at the hostel though. He drifted away into a daydream, smiling.

That night it seemed necessary to carefully hammer a block of wood into each of the right work boots of the three possible stucco pocket fillers. It gave a certain warmth to his soul as he tucked in tight against the icy night air.

The team was running a children's club daily. Originally this was planned to be held in a day–care centre very close to the build sites. However the centre manager had acted with an incredible lack of virtue; opting for a little small–scale racketeering rather than working with the grain of the group's desire to bless the community in which he lived.

There had been the beginnings of relationship developing in the last few years with the day–care centre, a modest rather run down premises. The teams had been allowed to use the land, which was of course ideal for a children's club. This had drawn the kids off the work sites, given them a fabulous time, and facilitated great community interaction for the build teams, which had run the club in groups of 12–15 or so, on rotation.

But the manager had started to make demands on the US non–profit this year. He wanted a church built. They painstakingly explained that there was a process by which any building would be done, and that began with asking church leaders in the community to own the assessment of needs criteria, and together decide which families would most benefit from housing. That had to be the focus. Furthermore, plans only existed for an appropriate house, and planning permission — difficult enough to gain in itself — was only at present given for the house plans they were currently using.

Discussion of construction of churches was a long way off, and all the other church leaders locally needed to be part of that discussion, and agree that it was a sufficient priority to divert resources and effort. It was clearly unlikely that this would be agreed anytime soon.

Without notice, on the morning of the first children's club, the use of the facility was withdrawn by the manager. The message was clear; you won't scratch my back, I won't scratch yours!

A quick re-think saw the club moved two blocks away to an 'orphanage' which was happy to help. Here Casper got some of his most significant insight into what was happening here in Botleng, both in the immediate community and through its impact on the wider area.

The orphanage was non-residential. Its existence was paid for and owned by the community around it. Everyone knew that people were dying, many from AIDS. This was leaving significant numbers of children without support and protection.

One of the teams was building a house for a family whose kids had been old enough to scrape through the child-led home stage when they lost their parents.

If the children had been any younger when their parents had died they would have been at high risk of dying themselves four weeks later — of starvation. This apparently happened in very many of the communities affected by deep poverty. Casper was discovering that life was harsh and its blows were cruel.

Here though, something wonderful was happening. Knowing that individually families could not support extra children, the community had come together to arrange what was possible. The children were housed overnight with families that had sufficient room to put them under cover. During the day, they were fed and taught by the orphanage workers, many of whom were volunteers. The whole project was paid for by the local churches and the people living nearby, who were mainly in very poor housing themselves. It was a beautiful picture of grace and mercy in an extremely hard situation.

On Casper's day of children's club duty, the team bus arrived outside the orphanage 30 minutes before the start time. They planned to spend those 30 minutes going through the programme, dividing up the tasks and so on. However almost immediately, around 70 children swarmed around the vehicle and began to rock it.

"I guess we'll start now then!" proclaimed Jim; the jolly Irish, guitar–playing children's team coordinator.

When the official start time swept by, 120 highly excited kids were broken into six smaller groups, rotating around creative, sporty, storytelling and musical activities. It was simply wonderful to play with the kids. Casper could have done this all week. Until now he had not noticed his own skills in this area. He hadn't had much to do with children before. He lost a big chunk of his heart to the kids in that orphanage.

But life during this trip was not confined to manual building work, children's clubs and educational input. These were British young people on an adventure, and their leaders had considerable expertise in understanding what was important to them.

Consequently, on Tuesday evening Casper had been amused to observe the English party cope with watching the FIFA World Cup being held in Brazil.

He hadn't been able to help himself accidentally dropping into the conversation that the USA had gone further in the competition than England. Despite their early exit, the English were still hugely interested in the tournament.

The final was between Germany and Argentina, which presented a problem for his British friends. Who to support? The 'Hand-of-God, Falklands-invading Argies' or the Germans, historic rivals and cause of more England football fans' pain than any other team? The group was split right down the middle and the big screen atmosphere for the game was like an NFL grudge match, despite the fact that everyone in the room was a neutral. When the match was edged by Germany, there was a grudging admiration among all, for a superb young German side. It was surreal to be sitting in a darkened room on a freezing South African winter night grouped around a make-shift projector screen and caring about a game between two nations about which he knew little — half a world away.

Seeing professional sportsmen compete for what everyone except his countrymen acknowledged as the greatest sporting prize in the world, Casper began to reflect on his own life choices. A strong, quick, wide receiver with lightning reflexes, he had represented both SDSU and Dartmouth. Twice he had just missed all-American honours in school by a few yards. In his last year at Dartmouth, Scouts had come calling for him and made it clear that there was draft interest in him.

He had however declined the draft process and had chosen entrepreneurship over football. In the end, a bit of fame and cash were not enough of a challenge — and football was just a game. It had not been a difficult choice to make. The key factors had been about what gave him the greatest buzz — apart from his addictions, of course. He was a leader of men, interested in power and risk. He had known then and he knew now: enterprising leadership was where his future lay.

And here in South Africa, he could feel something enormous beckoning him. His life was certainly changing again. If this country was indicative of the whole continent then the need for strong leaders attracted to high risk, was huge. More importantly for someone wired like Casper, the outcomes could be strategically massive and positively impact vast numbers of people. Where others would slump their shoulders in despair at the vastness of the needs, Casper looked out at the lines of corrugated iron shacks and thought, 'Yes! Here is a proper mountain to climb. I have what it takes; a black American with money, skills, drive, charisma and nerve. I can do this!'

Casper had a lot of dying to do.

On a completely different track, on Wednesday Casper had glimpsed something astonishing and indeed for him, hair–raising.

It came at the end of what had been an incredible discourse by a highly distinguished financial expert on the subject of 'hearing God.' This dude, whose career had included disposing of Lehmann Brothers' assets, merging banks, being in the room reluctantly empowering Oligarchs following the breakup of the Soviet Union, and reporting directly to the Senate on matters of finance, was no lightweight in the economic world.

Casper was now wrestling with some of the most astounding claims he'd heard in some time, put so disarmingly naturally that they were extremely easy to digest. They included audibly hearing God shout, at one end of the spectrum, and observing life's circumstances and listening to faithful friends at the other. There was much for him to process. Only Rick spoke like this back home, and though Casper rated Rick very highly, on account of his remarkable missionary career he couldn't really be classified as 'normal.' Here was some big shot finance dude from Casper's own world talking in a similar language to his about God being properly accessible and knowable every day at work, rather than the vague concept brought out for acts of worship in Christian gatherings, which until now Casper and many of his peers kinda owned.

Sat down in his seat processing these earth–shattering thoughts and their implications, Casper was not particularly aware that the room was emptying as the kids and their leaders headed purposefully towards an enormous bonfire, the only decent heat–source on this penetratingly cold campus.

Seeing Laodicea

He glanced up as a thick-set leader, one of his main opponents in the prank and banter stakes, said, 'I think we ought to pray for your back.'

For a moment he thought he might be the object of the statement but, was relieved to follow the gaze of the speaker, which was fixed on a young female leader by the name of Leila. Another male leader from the group clearly made up the 'we' who were offering to pray.

Casper had noticed that the girl had been moving uneasily about the build site.

'Ok thanks' the girl responded. She didn't look overly keen, kinda reluctant and eager at the same time; almost not daring to hope but also hoping for a touch from God.

The two men knelt down beside the seated Leila and the older one, Andrew, looked into her eyes and reminded her of a couple of things. God was always for us, always kind, always loving; and despite these facts, that many people did not receive what they wanted from him. This was no indicator of his love or lack of it. His reasons for healing people were many and varied. His reasons for withholding healing were even less easy to comprehend and also many and varied.

Curiously Andrew reminded Leila that everyone Jesus healed had gone on to die of something else. Many people were not healed even when he was ministering. On occasions the bible records that 'everyone was healed' — but those occasions were fairly rare.

He then asked her what was wrong.

'I slipped a disc in my back 18 months ago and have been in almost constant pain ever since. It was a big factor in my reluctance to come on the trip. My back has been reasonably stable for a few months now and I didn't want to jolt it or aggravate the injury.'

The listeners quietly waited for more.

'On Monday I wrenched it sawing the panels. I have been in a lot of pain since then.' Leila's lip quivered but she controlled herself and continued. 'I have been taking pain killers and doing my best to carry on but it's getting the better of me. I may have to drop out altogether tomorrow and rest.'

'Let's pray for you then.'

The two men then each put a hand on Leila's arms and Andrew prayed aloud, commanding her back to come into line. After a short while he stopped praying.

'How does it feel?'

'No different really.' Leila said quietly.

'Can you stand up and stretch please, see if there has been an improvement.'

She did as requested.

'No improvement.' The disappointment was palpable.

'Then let's pray again.' There was something resigned about the way Andrew spoke. An air of implacable 'not giving up so easily, this is too important' about him.

They prayed again, exactly as before, not verbatim but the same sense. No more strident, no less authoritative.

Leila began to tremble and her right leg to shake. She became tearful, slightly shocked. She clearly felt something physical had happened but was not responding with a clichéd horror movie paranormal reaction that one might imagine. There was a gentle wonder in the room. The tears were of tenderness not of fear.

Slowly, carefully, without being asked, Leila stood to her feet. She was reluctant to weight bear because her back had been shaken by what had happened to her leg and she was in fear of a catastrophic collapse. When she did stand properly her expression relaxed and she look slightly perplexed.

'How does it feel?'

'The pain has gone.'

'Glory to God! Only God heals; don't forget to thank him!'

And with that, Andrew was gone. Casper slipped over to the bonfire with still more processing to do.

The two glimpses into the intimate presence of God he'd experienced this evening had left him unnerved, intrigued and hungry for more in a way that made him feel slightly guilty. It seemed like he'd been able to peer momentarily beyond some locked doors into a world others inhabited.

On this, the final evening before tomorrow's handover of the keys to their beautiful new homes, the trip leaders issued each participant a keepsake in the form of a key bearing the organisation's logo and the year 2014, suspended on a leather necklace.

'There's only one way in which you can get one of these,' explained Dick. 'You must get together the finances to pay your way and come either here or to Mexico and build a house for a family that desperately needs it.'

He had their attention.

'Some of you will wear this for many years; most of you will keep it safely maybe for the remainder of your lives as a permanent reminder of the joy and triumph you will feel tomorrow as you set a family free from housing poverty.

'Let it also remind you of two more things; While you have been here some of you have been set free from issues that have chained you for years. Others have received keys to open up doors which will set the future direction for your lives. Wear it, keep it, never forget and never go back to the way you were.'

The role of handing out keys was not given to some dignitary. This task went to a young man of around 18 from Casper's build team. He'd spent almost all week mixing stucco. First to start, last to stop, he'd impressed the American. In the past, this young man had vowed that a previous key he'd received would not be his last. It seemed appropriate that one for whom the keys had such significant meaning should award them to the others. It added something.

Casper got his key, and confided to old Blair that he too would be wearing it for some time to come.

He and Blair had managed one meal together while on the trip. Again he had been struck by the fierce intelligence coupled with an exuberant *joie de vivre* in the fellow. He was older than he looked, and kept himself in shape. He read constantly, so held very current and coherent views on global trends, theological and political opinion, and technology. Casper felt like he'd found a friend, despite not knowing him at all well (apart from some early unexpected intimacy on the office carpet).

Blair had shown him around the quarter where the teams were building, and introduced him to a group from an international pharmaceutical company based in Massachusetts called Livelife Pharma, with a subsidiary here in Johannesburg. The Livelife team, wearing brick red teeshirts emblazoned with a rather energetic–looking cartoon heart logo complete with arms and legs, sold medicines to assist the circulatory system. These guys, all aged between 25 and 35, were sales reps on a teambuilding exercise, were also busily applying stucco to a home within the Botleng Township.

Casper, already something of a self–proclaimed expert in stucco application, helped himself to a hawk and used it to get alongside a particularly pretty young sales rep, Bonnie. Of course he had somewhat mixed motives. It was not hard to justify a conversation with a vivacious young white saleswoman about how she had come to be working for a poverty–stricken black family. It turned out that Bonnie had just joined the company and this was her first "sales conference." She'd thought 'bring a pair of

Seeing Laodicea

gardening shoes or boots' in the instructions had been for an optional exercise she could escape. They glanced down simultaneously at her heeled black velour power-dressing court shoes, pulled faces at each other and giggled.

'I have never set foot in a township before. I honestly thought I'd be assaulted if I ever did so. Coming here has been a big eye-opener. There's a whole lot of need and all but I see people caring for one another. The orphanage down the road where you guys have been holding your children's club for example — it's just wonderful. I hadn't imagined people could be so community minded. Wouldn't happen in my neighbourhood.'

Casper was impressed by what she said, but he was more interested in the impact Blair's little outfit was having on her subliminally. Here was a pharmaceutical distribution company sending its people into what they thought might be a hostile environment to do something good, as part of a bonding exercise. The employees were discovering some things about their own prejudices, about poverty and about how people they had been brought up to hate had things to teach them. The ripples of what was happening here were going out sure enough. As with the pastors who came in to speak over dinner, Casper was learning as much from what was not intentionally said as from what was stated.

He had a growing understanding now of the work of Blair's nonprofit. It benefitted churches by empowering them to make a difference to the chronic housing problems in their communities. It made a difference to participants in its trips. It made a life changing difference to families trapped by poverty in inadequate, dangerous and disease-inducing housing by the cruel grip of poverty. It was causing two divided communities to find one another here in South Africa. This happy-go-lucky genius of a man — to whom the world appeared to be a place to be enjoyed — had almost none of the skills so valued by his world, and yet the impact of his life was incredible.

Casper felt there was something happening, that he wasn't seeing. He was only noticing the effects of it. He was reminded of how Leila had been healed right in front of him. He was seeing and yet there was something out of sight — out of his experience. Maybe it was something values-based, found in and around these people; a way of being that was transformative, potent — dangerous in a trustworthy kind of a way.

It was almost as if an unused sense in him had picked up on something. Like any decent scientist, he was starting to follow the evidence. It was pointing into the unknown but not necessarily the unknowable. Right there on a tiny plot in the middle of a sprawling desperate township an unknown girl had helped show him something she herself couldn't see. She, along with a wide range of disparate people, had handed him some keys.

Seeing Laodicea

8.   HIDDEN

Benjamin sat in his Ouagadougou office, impatiently tapping his gold plated Mont Blanc pen on the crisp luxurious top sheet of the leather bound desk pad which sat on his expansive mahogany desk.

Smartly, and slightly ostentatiously dressed, intelligently good looking in his Hugo Boss gold rimmed half framed glasses — he was every inch the highly–qualified professional. If you wanted something organised in Sub–Saharan Africa, then everyone knew that the man to contact was Benjamin Traoré.

On the screen of his MacBook Air was yet another email from an increasingly impatient Casper Scales.

What to do? That was Benjamin's dilemma. He was drawn to the obvious pot of gold which the naïve young American so clearly wanted to pass on. He was also extremely concerned by the potential hazard posed by Pastor Joseph Oudraogo.

It would not be difficult to eliminate this threat the same way as he had disposed of Joseph's father. The complicating factor was that Benjamin had been warned of an enquiry relating to whether he had ever been employed by Light to Africa. That enquiry he suspected came from the office of a subsidiary of CaMPuS Solutions Inc.

As luck would have it, one of his old nursing team was still employed there and had replied to the contrary. For now his tail was covered. More contact with the Oudraogos would increase the risk of further questions being asked.

No, Mister Scales could not be allowed to unpick his veneer of respectability in the USA. A tempting mark he may be, but not tempting enough to risk upsetting a highly lucrative system.

Silencing Africans had so far proven simple enough; but an American — and a rich powerful one at that — might prove too much of a challenge.

He sighed regretfully and, ever the decisive executive, assigned the email to the recycle bin and blocked the sender. He could not afford the risk.

His brilliant mind turned to the immediate tasks of the day. Here at the National HQ of United Medical in Burkina Faso, he was busy conducting a review of performance statistics relating to the distribution of medicines and mosquito nets.

He was particularly interested in anti–retroviral medicines benevolently provided by a large European distributor. He had an elegant double–supply operation in place.

A Chinese manufacturer was producing herbal vitamin supplements designed to look identical in every way to the European anti–retroviral drugs.

An Indian printing company was responsible for producing packaging for the Chinese medicine identical to that of the European HIV treatments.

By a clever warehousing operation in which he varied the racks from which supplies were taken, he was able to halve the delivery of legitimate drugs, supplied in good faith almost free of charge to needy Africans by the Europeans. He substituted them for his Chinese vitamins, incorrectly labeled.

The problem, from a patient's perspective, with the herbal medicine produced in China, was that it was utterly useless at inhibiting progress towards the worst complications of HIV and the development of AIDS. This was not Benjamin's problem and therefore didn't concern him.

For audit cover, a ghost NGO was ordering, and could show distribution records for the vitamin supplements. Inexpensive vitamin supplements attracted little interest from medical auditors. Nobody had ever checked out this NGO, which Benjamin ironically labeled The M. Celeste Foundation.

The outcome of his supply strategy was that he could still demonstrate some efficacy of medical intervention to those in need in Burkina Faso, while receiving a generous income from the Parisian black market for deliveries of expensive anti–retroviral medicines re–routed by Benjamin to French distributors. The prices paid to him by the Paris–based operators were excellent.

The Burkina Faso operation was just one of seven. He duplicated this activity in Senegal, the Gambia, Mali, Chad, South Sudan and Niger. Benjamin's operations were primarily in the Sahel Belt, a semi–arid demarcation of Sub–Saharan Africa, constantly in danger of famine and the worst ravages of poverty. It was an ideal place to run his various scams. There were so many agencies motivated to address the problems in the region that the chaos caused by competing clamours for help gave plenty of room for the bogus among the legitimate.

As he had done all his life, Benjamin sailed as close to the wind as possible and at every stage ensured that his back was covered. The pace and the scale of his plans were such that he constantly kept ahead of any suspicions in the same way as a good conjuror feigns magic. Nobody could imagine that anyone would go to this amount of trouble, move at such speed or make such

Seeing Laodicea

awesome arrangements — thus the only thing to be believed was what he showed.

Most of the operatives in his schemes were unaware of any other part of the setup. It was a very neat and strategically pleasing labyrinth and Benjamin was beyond brilliant at running it. He was its hub, its defender and its architect. The organigram that gave the overview of his true programme of operations was held on this MacBook only, and was double-encrypted within a file held in an "Old Instruction Manuals" folder under his Documents tree. The file itself was a small pdf document, something that would not attract the attention of a hacker. It held the locations and the hyper-links needed to reach them, of all the various statistical reports produced by his numerous isolated departments. From these he tracked and archived his profit reports, which were impressive.

Benjamin smiled craftily. It was the 'one file to rule them all, and in the darkness bind them.' He smiled — he loved Tolkien.

He had an office here in Ouagadougou that he visited fairly frequently because the hub of his Parisian supply chain was located here. However his preferred place of operation was at Serrekunda on the Atlantic coast of the Gambia. Travel around the region was conducted by charter aircraft, paid for by United Medical. He planned to head off to Banjul and on to Serrekunda after church tomorrow. Prior to leaving the office Benjamin had a couple of things to tighten up.

Inoussa Hamidou, head of station here in Burkina Faso, had completed seven years of service. Benjamin had come to rely upon Hamidou's excellent skills — particularly his ability to unquestioningly follow orders. Notwithstanding the good working relationship the two men enjoyed, there was one small issue that had arisen. Hamidou, in common with so many of his countrymen had a tendency to employ his own family. In order to do so, it had been necessary for him to engineer the departure of an incumbent of a post from time to time. This was achieved in a variety of ways but Hamidou's preference was to make life so difficult for his chosen target that they would find it impossible to remain in employment.

For the last five weeks Raogo Sawadogo a decent enough clerk, but unfortunately from the wrong family — had been forced to work in a concrete block building with a corrugated iron roof, used previously as a store. With no electricity supply Raogo had no fan or aircon available and the temperature within the building rose during the heat of the day to 48–52°C. Sawadogo's inevitable complaint had fallen on deaf ears. He had changed his working hours to early in the morning and late in the evening, to avoid the heat. He could not afford to lose the job. He would do anything to complete his work even if it meant splitting the shift and catching up sleep in the middle of the day. His work had suffered slightly as he made the adjustment.

Then had come the change in delivery schedules imposed from above. He was required to complete and file his returns by 4 p.m. each day. The implications of this were that he could not complete the task without facing the heat. It was only a matter of time before he quit. Nobody could survive those conditions for long.

Raogo Sawadogo would stick in there as long as possible. He was responsible not only for his own family but also his twin sister Poko's. Soon after he had got her a job with United Medical, Poko's husband had mentioned that their family was in need and hungry. This had sounded innocent enough but Raogo knew that if he were to refuse to carry them, the consequences could be disastrous. Poko and her husband would be sure to approach the shaman and a ju would be put on Raogo, causing him any of a range of ills. He had taken them in.

Raogo's task was to produce manifest reports for supplies shipped daily out to the provinces. These were taken to the bus station on any of a number of decrepit trucks, clearly labeled for their onward destination depot. In order for this work to be done discretely, Raogo knew more than most about how Benjamin's system worked here in Burkina Faso. He had been in post long before Benjamin had taken control, and was a bright and hard working administrator. He was aware of the distribution changes Benjamin had brought to the organisation and was paid not to mention their implications. He was vital to Benjamin's concealment arrangements. Inoussa Hamidou had picked the wrong target.

Benjamin spoke with flat finality to Hamidou.

'I am transferring your brother to Tenkodougou where our team needs strengthening. He will become head of station there. You will need to make arrangements for him to pass on his responsibilities. He will leave in four weeks.'

Hamidou was stunned.

'In the meantime ensure that Raogo Sawadogo is upgraded to take responsibility for all administration of distribution. I am very impressed with his efficiency, particularly in his ability to operate in the conditions under which you have placed him.'

Hamidou's perplexity now turned to fear. Benjamin had a reputation for looking after certain favourites within the organisation. Raogo Sawadogo had never been noticeable as one of them. Hamidou's mind raced to review how he had treated Sawadogo, understanding now that he must have crossed a line with Benjamin. He could expect no mercy. Benjamin was not a man to be reasoned with. Those who questioned his decisions were out of the organisation instantly. Benjamin's rule was one of fear, his lieutenants — including Hamidou — knew that one step out of line could mean termination both in terms of employment, and with regard to accidents that had been known to occur to those dismissed soon after leaving.

His shoulders sagged in defeat as he accepted this catastrophic turn of events from his brother's perspective. There would be relatives in Tenko and it would be possible for the wider family to adapt to the disastrous employment change. Adaptability towards disaster was a strength possessed by the Dyula tribe.

Benjamin had one final menacing statement to make.

'You have become emboldened by successfully driving out members of the Mossi tribe from the organisation. This policy may not have upheld the best interests of United Medical. I think it is time to redress the balance a little. In future, when you are thinking of making arrangements for the constructive dismissal of key employees you would do well to consult me before taking any action.'

The interview was over.

Benjamin was a welcome sight at the Deliverance Church of Christ, in prosperous Secteur 15 of Ouagadougou. He had held a leadership position in the denomination for some years and was seen very much as a "leader at large" within the movement.

People looked up to him. His power and influence obtained things for the church and gave its other leaders a certain gravitas when speaking with officials. He was also a most generous donor. Benjamin had found that in every church he attended — and there were many — money almost invariably bought leadership influence.

He had found that church leaders, especially in the more affluent churches, tended to take a very different view of Christian behaviour within the leadership team from that which was projected onto their congregations. After all they argued, the Apostle Paul himself had stated that it was the weaker Christians who abstained from certain foods, didn't drink wine, respected special days and so on. If you felt that something you were doing was not wrong, however dubious; so long as you kept it to yourself and didn't cause the weak to stumble, that was allowable.

This policy allowed Benjamin to explain himself when he was occasionally exposed by an indulgence; a cigar in the wrong company; one too many Jack Daniels and so on. There was a superiority of education and overseas learning to Benjamin that gave him enough gravitas at points of tension, and church leaders overlooked indiscretions on the grounds that they themselves were possibly being over-judgmental.

Seeing Laodicea

He was of course careful to mask anything which was beyond the grey areas of nuanced interpretation, which the church at any level would rule out. He did not modify his tastes, he increased his concealments.

This morning's service began as usual with a prolonged prayer time to which the zealous were expected to attend. Here "demons" were cast out of everything from djembes to joists. There was generally enough "binding" going on to start a small printing company.

The main service would begin with someone loud, standing to sing lustily at the microphone and a steady influx of the faithful would go on for the next hour or so. Musicians would arrive, strap on a guitar or pick up their percussion piece and join in, tuning their instruments as they went. The cacophony produced was wonderfully rhythmic, tonally disastrous, loud, proud, and provided the perfect foundation for exuberant worship — combining ululation, shouting, screaming and singing. It was easily the most entertaining way to spend a Sunday morning, and Benjamin always loved it.

When it came time for giving to the church, the congregants danced to the front in jubilation as they theatrically tossed their tithes and then their offerings into separate collection baskets. The worship leader ensured that the maximum possible emphasis was given to this part of the worship, urging the people to excel in the grace of giving.

'For with the measure you use, you shall receive!' he cried fervently, urgently, 'You shall not fail to receive back 100 times more than you have given!'

Giving was something the congregation enjoyed, and each gave with an expectation of blessing that lifted them up out of their poverty and filled them with anticipation. They dreamed of better and placed their hope in God, their offerings invested in that hope. Jubilation and celebration characterised this time. Benjamin himself was as always caught up in it, and danced his way down the aisle, tossing a considerable wad into each basket.

Nowhere near a tenth of his income went into the tithe basket but it was nonetheless impressive and who would know?

Today the Most Reverend Founding Apostolic Father Elijah Kormea, an ex–pat from Sierra Leone was responsible for the sermon. Resplendent in gold–braided African formal dress, he harangued all and sundry with blurted statements pulled from all over the Bible, linked loosely with his theme of blessing.

Much of his discourse depended on the force of his personality, and the congregation swayed and responded enthusiastically as his tone demanded.

His sermon reached a well choreographed and oft repeated crescendo.

'Abraham: rich or poor?' He shouted.

'Rich!' responded the faithful.

'Isaac: rich or poor?'

'Rich!'

'Jacob: rich or poor?'

'Rich!'

'Joseph: rich or poor?'

'Rich!'

'David: rich or poor?'

'Rich!'

'Solomon: rich or poor?'

'Rich!'

Seeing Laodicea

'My brothers, Jehovah's blessing does not leave you in poverty. He has the power to make you rich! He wants to make you rich! A sure sign of the blessing of God is that you will become rich, as children of the God who owns the cattle on a thousand hills you can expect to be rich!'

There followed a time of ministry where congregants were invited to come forward for prayer. Prayer ministry was conducted loudly and with great fervour.

'Ibrahim what are you seeking God for? How do you want him to bless you?'

'I am wanting to buy a taxi, Apostle. I want to start a taxi business.'

'God is saying that he does not want you to have a taxi; he wants you to have twelve taxis and drivers and an office. He wants to bless you brother. He wants to pour out his goodness on you. He wants you to know his extravagant grace and love. Hallelujah! Praise his mighty name, amen, AMEN!'

The apostle pushed Ibrahim, who was swaying in ecstatic joy, sending him gratefully, tearfully to his knees. Founding Apostolic Father Elijah then promptly moved swiftly along to the next eager petitioner.

There would be no taxi. There would only be continued grinding poverty.

But there would be hope for a time, and that hope would keep the "revolving door" congregation coming through it — eager for their itching ears to hear what was pleasing.

Probably the saddest part of the whole excited affair was that everyone believed it was good and true, including Founding Apostolic Father Elijah Kormea. He was simply passing on what he had been taught, and was building a successful church as instructed by his apostolic oversight.

Somehow despite his education and some well-formed opinions, the superstitious elements of Benjamin's nature still kept him putting money into the offering, and he felt a strange massage to some personal spiritual hunger from the platitudinous nonsense that was preached. 'It may be a circus' he mused, but it is a circus I enjoy attending.

Somehow it afforded him the opportunity to attend church without any dangerous side effects like conviction. It was church on his terms, and he could afford it. Besides it was important for building a trustworthy persona. It was well worth a few thousand in donations, to keep the multi-million dollar wheels of his fraudulent empire turning.

After the service Benjamin discreetly visited his second wife Fatouma, a nubile grateful Mossi girl whom he'd rescued from his favourite massage parlour. Her dependence on him was a huge power trip well worth the cost of the relationship's indulgence. Always grateful, she was utterly faithful to him and willing at any time to do anything for him, at any time — anything.

Fatouma was one of several such relationships he enjoyed. His one legitimate marriage had ended in an acrimonious and potentially costly divorce. Then had come an unfortunate acid attack followed within eighteen months by her suicide before the courts could decide on settlement of assets. His first and only true love, turned to hate.

Satisfactorily fed and post coitally fatigued, Benjamin made his way to Ouagadougou airport where his chartered flight awaited him. The flight time to Banjul was less than two hours.

Benjamin, along with executives of many other agencies, now took charter flights with a small and comparatively well organised private outfit for journeys between countries in Central and West Africa.

Sweating overland from Ouagadougou to Serrekunda would mean 24–36 hours and would include multiple stops — especially along the cursed South Bank road through the Gambia. Here

Seeing Laodicea

police check points abounded and biting insects predated on the vulnerable vehicle occupants, feasting at will while the officer had a leisurely flick through the presented documents. Benjamin was convinced that the blood of travelers at checkpoints formed an important constituent of the official lifecycle of a good proportion of the insect population along the road.

By late evening Benjamin, was by–passing the customs and immigration hall at Banjul airport, slipping into his spacious white Toyota Land Cruiser Prado. This luxury 4x4 ironed out the bumps along the Banjul–Serrekunda highway. Turning into Kairaba Avenue, Benjamin dropped in as he always did, at La Parisian Café opposite the American embassy. He was pleased to catch up with his Libyan friends there and enjoy a decent coffee.

Ensuring that he bought a bag full of oranges and bananas from atop the head of a little girl outside the café — an important inexpensive show of benevolence — he headed down to Atlantic Boulevard and on to his delightful rented Fajara house just along from the British Embassy overlooking the sea.

Tucked behind beautiful flowering shrubs and a high wall was Benjamin's hideaway. Here his comely girlfriend Aminata awaited him. Most people thought she was his wife, mainly because he always introduced her as such. He and Aminata had been together for around four years. She had been a hostess over at the seaside resort of Senegambia, a favourite haunt for officers of NGOs. Aminata was happy to be whoever he told her to be.

He was away much of the time and she was free to spend those days with her friends and family. She no longer wondered where her next meal would come from, never had to entertain drunken feral clients, lived in paradise, spent pretty much what she liked and drove a Range Rover Evoque. The relationship — if that was what it was — worked like so many of Benjamin's arrangements; an elegant solution. It met their mutual physical needs and had nothing to do with love.

Neither could expose their true feelings for the other, those must remain forever hidden. Intimacy was impossible. Two people cohabiting left both with obligations. For Aminata, sexual activity was a showcase, every time. She felt obliged to perform, aware always that with regard to this beautiful house; her tenure was fragile. He knew that if his financial empire fell apart, she would instantly be gone, in search of another sugar daddy.

That night they lay together as they often did — unclad, physically together, emotionally separate, unmarried; with no covenant of peace, apart.

Seeing Laodicea

9.　DAYLIGHT

Candice and Prity emerged from Sardar Vallabhbhai Patel International Airport, Ahmedabad and were immediately greeted by clamouring taxi drivers. The drivers crowded back behind an invisible line waving and jostling, seeking fares. A stern looking policeman brandishing an impressive baton stood between them and the straggle of incoming passengers who were emerging from baggage reclaim. Occasionally the enthusiasm of the drivers overcame their restraint and the police officer would move swiftly to drive them back. Once behind the invisible line he'd drawn, the pressure to obtain a fare steadily mounted until the group jostled forward again and the officer was obliged to get involved once more. An uneasy dynamic equilibrium had thus been established.

The two women had no need of a cab. A grinning Ravi Christi, now based in Ahmedabad, marched them to a battered Mahindra 4x4. Bags loaded, Ravi launched the vehicle in among the crazy traffic of the bustling city.

Despite a degree of familiarity with Asian driving gained in Vietnam, and some experience moving around during the

Seeing Laodicea

conference in Kerala, Candice had to shut her eyes. The driving here in Gujarat State was simply terrifying. Brakes were seldom used here — the horn, steering and lightning reflexes were the all-important elements of survival. Conformance to traffic regulations was unthinkable. You just went out there and threaded your vehicle through every conceivable gap at maximum possible speed. No American could drive here. Candice would have caused chaos by braking and giving way; something none of the other drivers would expect and would therefore be totally unprepared for such unprecedented eccentricity.

Somewhat relieved to be intact Candice alighted at a Methodist hostel which was largely unoccupied and complete with stray dogs running loose along the landings. It wasn't quite the Waldorf Astoria, but it had a shower, a flushing toilet and only cost around $3 per night; well within her budget for as long as she wanted to stay. The mattress was lumpy and thin, but with two more unoccupied beds in the room to raid, three of them made quite a decent place to lay and stretch out.

Candice was staying here alone. Prity had a room in the CKK team base where she'd lived for some time. While Prity went over there and got settled back in, Candice unpacked and freshened up. She had a couple of hours to spare, so strolled across the road to a little stall, ordering a coffee with only a small degree of difficulty. The coffee came only one way; made with buffalo milk, sweet, small and reasonably strong. It cost her eight rupees, or 12 cents.

Prity arrived right on time to pick her up, tossing her a crash helmet and gesturing for Candice to jump on the back of her scooter. If the car ride had been terrifying, zipping through the nightmare traffic on a scooter was unbelievable.

Candice had to keep her eyes open in order to discern which way to lean. This would not have been her preference, as it forced her to notice and respond to the incredible world of Ahmedabad's traffic.

There was a certain pecking order — a caste system if you like — to the rights of way. At the very top were cows to which everything gave way. Then came lorries and buses, big and battered, equipped with impressive horns; then minibuses, vans, big old cars, big new cars, little old cars, little new cars, motorised rickshaws, van rickshaws, pedal rickshaws, scooters, and bicycles. Pedestrians made their way across roads at their own peril, and much as for cows, the maniacal traffic flowed around them. The sound of the traffic was utter bedlam.

Candice prayed comically, childishly, continuously, arriving at the CKK team base shaken and shocked. This was now to be her daily routine until they could move up towards Palanpur, the chosen base for the Hunger to Wholeness and CKK economic development partnership to take place.

Once in the converted house, Candice was introduced to the local team — mainly young people on internships and undergraduate theology and discipleship courses. Everyone was amazingly friendly, anxious to make her feel welcome.

When it came time to eat, a modest and very tasty vegetarian curry was served with wonderful roti. It was nourishing healthy food — something Candice found most encouraging. Team conversation over lunch quickly became boisterous. Although she had no idea of what was being said she enjoyed the gaiety and laughter that billowed around the kitchen and yard. These were happy people.

Candice was not permitted to wash her dish or cutlery. She protested but was overpowered. It would take a little while before she could properly fit in and do her share.

The first days were mainly devoted to introductions, making embryonic organisational beginnings and initial planning arrangements for the future.

First they needed a name which remained neutral between both organisations and would make sense in a Western market. Candice was very clear on how she wanted to proceed. In the

Seeing Laodicea

USA there would be no caste recognition except where they were dealing with people of sub–continental origin. The term Dalit would hold no stigma there. In fact exposing the plight of the Dalits and making a commercial response would be a significantly positive brand statement.

They chose the name Dälight, pronounced 'Daylight'.

The setup process began by reviewing their values. Candice was convinced that having a set of values that people could be held to was far more preferable than writing reams of procedures and rules stating expectations.

To arrive at the project's values they started with two lists. First they listed the things they would live for; the things that brought them alive. They asked questions like: 'What gets us up in the morning? What keeps us up late at night?'

They looked at the Christian manifesto read aloud by Christ himself; he being the living foundation of the church on which their efforts towards the elimination of poverty would be built. Candice quoted from one of her Pacific Professors.

> 'There is no other foundation worth building upon than Christ. Building on your own history or that of someone else who's seen success or on organisational preferences in response to current cultural trends is the precursor to posting demolition notices.'

They read together the account in the Gospel of Luke, Chapter 4, listing the benefits of the Kingdom whose inception had first been drafted 600 years earlier, proclaimed authoritatively by Jesus Christ at the start of his ministry.

Then, after considerable discussion they scripted the formal basis for everything they would go on to do.

The Essence of Dälight Gujarat Is:

Dälight brings hope to the hopeless by manifesting the justice, humility and kindness of Jesus Christ.

Dälight Gujarat would rather die than forsake:

- *Agape love; all people will be precious to us.*
- *The values of Christ as revealed in the bible.*
- *The presence of God visible in our actions.*
- *Integrity; we will be who we say we are.*

Everything Dälight Gujarat does will be:

- *In the interest of those affected by poverty as our first priority.*
- *Collaborative, globally, with local churches.*
- *Of the highest quality, on time, and fairly rewarded.*
- *Environmentally responsible.*

After prayer, the first two staff members of Dälight Gujarat committed themselves to own its values. This was the essence to which they would always call one another to account, along with anyone that joined them.

Prity was exceptionally quick witted and once they had put together a draft plan of action, within 48 hours she had formed a schedule and budget for public transport, visits, networking meetings and discussions with Gujarati Scheduled Caste, OBC and Dalit community leaders.

Already Candice was starting to understand the wisdom of HWI in choosing to always work in partnership with well organised church networks that shared similar values regarding social justice. (She had heard in her training that there were plenty of organisations that labeled themselves "Church" and had absolutely no interest whatsoever in pursuing agendas of social justice. It was apparently important to HWI to move slowly and choose their new partners carefully.)

With Prity in the mix Candice immediately had access to priceless information that it would have taken a lifetime to acquire.

Seeing Laodicea

Dälight's work was to help Dalit women in particular to earn significantly better incomes than was currently possible by the process of economic development in rural Gujarat.

Of particular excitement to Candice was the thought of families being lifted by their own efforts into genuine sustainable economic stability — even prosperity. But she was unsure of how to land her thoughts, feeling nervous and inadequate. She did have big ideas though — terrifyingly big ideas. For now they would remain unspoken. She needed to understand the lie of the land before she started thinking about changes.

For Prity, the main excitement came from being able to work first among the people who had been so kind to her in Palanpur. She was thrilled by having the chance to transform their homes, clothing, educational aspirations, medical treatment and even their diet.

They took the bus up to Palanpur. Arrangements inside the vehicle were unusual. There were little booths attached to the ceiling, as well as seats below. Candice and Prity shared a booth, able to stretch out top–to–tail in the hot dusty bus. The curtains on the sunny side kept out some of the heat, but it was a terribly uncomfortable journey. Opening the windows let in the dust. It was a trade–off between choking and overheating. Fortunately for both girls, the well–travelled Prity ensured she selected the shadier side of the vehicle, thus their experience was cooler and the curtains did not need to be drawn. Candice was able to watch as they threaded their way through the frantic traffic flowing round little islands of serenely pacing cows.

On the pavements and road islands partially shaded by flyovers and the shadows of tall buildings and road signs, sun scorched people dressed in rags slept on filthy blankets. The dust and fumes from the traffic blew over them constantly. Prity explained that their houses were like ovens during the day, heating to over 50 degrees. These people were night workers who needed to sleep and out in the open was the only possible place. Oblivious to the cacophony of Ahmedabad's manic vehicles honking, ringing, revving and shouting their way past, these people somehow managed to catch their rest.

Candice and Prity were met at a junction bus station near the border. Here the village women sold their vegetables and artisans their crafts. It was a busy noisy fascinating place. Candice could have stayed and browsed for hours, but their lift awaited them. She found herself and her bags jammed into the back of a nondescript 60s-style car of indeterminate vintage. It was clearly very well cared for and shone with the polished gleam born of much conscientious effort.

After a visit to the bathroom to freshen up, Candice sat down with Prity and Avi to eat a formal dinner. Food at the fairly palatial Victorian–era mission station that was to be their base was divine. Avi's wife Rena was a superb cook, who knowing that she had a western visitor, had specially prepared chicken and chips.

Candice enquired if the salad had been washed with filtered water, her training surfacing in practice. Avi responded quickly:

'We use the salads in order to check that our filter is working properly. We will be monitoring your health closely for the next 24 hours.'

Candice chuckled, she was among friends. There were some delicious items in the salad that she did not recognise. Fresh produce abounded in this wonderful Eden. She was to discover that this meal in no way outshone those which would follow in the days ahead.

Prity was aware of how to best make contact with women who might be prepared to work together in a form of cooperative — or better still a small registered company. She was very well acquainted with the movers and shakers among the communities and families around Palanpur. She got right down to local arrangements, making calls and sending messages. Before long they had a long list of people to see.

Seeing Laodicea

A whirlwind tour of villages and the families within them gave Candice a much clearer idea of the lives of subsistence farmers. Images passed through her mind, filled with fresh information and sights as she lay down to sleep each night. Weathered faces creased by hardship regarded her inscrutably. Calloused hands lightly manipulated tools with the quick dexterity and economy of movement wrought by hard experience. Neat outbuildings containing beautifully kept animals, and irrigation channels watering chick peas, onions, brassicas and herbs in neat rows evidenced excellent land skills.

Women were always beautifully and modestly dressed. Even working the fields they wore their bright coloured silks. Candice could easily pick out the splashes of vibrant reds, pinks, yellows and rich blues of their saris sprinkled across the landscape.

Old worn implements, cracked crockery, spotless floors, ramshackle but tidy homes filled with happy people whose backs were bent by their labour filled her eyes.

The people worked hard. It was their way of life. Here you did not see the tea–drinking groups of men found gathering on the streets in the slums of Vietnam. During daylight hours, everyone was working. As light fell, the families gathered to eat simple beautiful and exquisitely flavoured foods. The fields produced an abundance of crops as these tough, wiry people worked their land with excellence.

HWI — and therefore by partnership Dälight — decided to offer a range of courses stimulating artisan–based small businesses. Delivered initially by short term specialist teams based in the USA, HWI had passed training delivery to a Delhi based indigenous unit. They in turn had picked up some government funded sponsorship and ran training for trainers in various states.

Candice was very keen to work alongside the HWI Gurujat team and was looking forward to connecting with them in a few weeks back in Ahmedabad. She had been warned by Rosalyn, her "Head of India" line manager back in the USA, that there were problems with the HWI Gujarat team. Apparently a lot of training was happening, but information on the success of the arising businesses was patchy and unreliable. Candice had been asked to improve this flow of information, the absence of which was leaving holes in their communications to donors.

Setting up a partnership with the Dalit church network was another huge priority. Here in Palanpur the CNI setup was the obvious base for their operations. Avi and Rena's work among the Tribals was fabulous and deeply appreciated. There were some questions she wanted answered regarding the integration of Dalit families into the churches. Christian discipleship in this context included abandoning cultural norms, however deeply ingrained, that were inhumane.

The fact that all Christians here were treated as Tribals was very positive for Dalit integration, and the recent history between Hindu and Christian families had seen a deeply held respect for the churches form within the culture. Thus Dalit families would find it easier than usual to follow Jesus. Candice was hopeful that with KCC input, existing CNI culture here, and HWI investment and opportunities something really fabulous would happen.

For now she was fact finding and assessing the opportunities that arose from key people with abilities by the state border, so far unconnected with HWI's efforts elsewhere in the state.

There was considerable talent in the local villages. Many of the women were able to dye cloth, weave and sew. They could make baskets and produce simple ornaments and jewellery from polished stone and wire.

Everything they produced was brightly coloured, and delightful. Much of it was sold to traders at the bus stations, some directly to tourists. Nobody was making huge profits and there was no sense of collaborative organisation. Candice looked at the bright, busy scene and was encouraged by the possibilities open to this clever group of people who were rich with cunning skills.

Candice had one particular delight awaiting her. It began early on day two. The previous evening, one young man named

Seeing Laodicea

Rachid, resident at the mission property, asked her if she would like a shower in the morning. She would later learn that Rachid was an adopted child of Rena and Avi.

She awoke to the sound of a crackling fire and an aromatic smell of wood smoke. She rubbed then focused a bleary eye, trying to make sense of what had disturbed her in the half–light of dawn. Through the ground floor window of her room she saw Rachid busily fanning a bonfire to flame. On checking her watch she groaned: 5:30 a.m. — what kind of a time was that to be building bonfires? She rolled over and drifted back into a light snooze.

A thud and splash followed by a sharp rap on her door startled her back into wakefulness. She checked her watch again: 6:30 a.m. — a slightly more respectable time but still antisocially early for a caller.

'Who is it?' she demanded. There was no reply, so she investigated and on opening the door discovered not a person but a pail of steaming hot water with a blue plastic jug floating at the top.

'Ooh I get it; the shower!' She murmured suddenly awake, pleased.

'Thanks!' She called shrilly.

The water was close to boiling, so Candice mixed it with some from the one tap in the bath room. The water in the pail smelled strongly of cold remedy. Rachid had added eucalyptus leaves to the water to make a pungent infusion.

As she poured the brownish aromatic fluid over her shapely frame, Candice reflected on the understated way in which she had been offered her shower. Rachid had risen at 5:00 am, collected firewood and built a fire. Then he had drawn water from the well, collected and added aromatic leaves from at least two different types of tree and suspended the mixture in a large pot above the hot fire. Finally he had transferred the resulting brew to a plastic bucket, added a jug for pouring, and carried it to her room, not even pausing to receive her thanks. She was genuinely humbled as her body shivered with pleasure, the hot stinging concoction splashing across her skin. She was slightly aghast at her careless response to last night's suggestion. She had put Rachid to a great deal of trouble. She was humbled.

After two weeks in Palanpur — where far too much of their time was spent playing with the girls in Prity's old orphanage, having gleaned enough information to begin to make a start — Candice and Prity returned to Ahmedabad.

Contact was made with HWI, who had now returned from the mission that had taken them out of the city the last time Candice was there. Prity picked up from the initial telephone call that all was not particularly friendly in the HWI office.

Her intuition was confirmed at the first meeting with the Ahmedabad Head of Station. Gull Batia — herself a Lohana, a merchant caste — made it abundantly clear that an uninvited American poking into her fiefdom was extremely unwelcome.

She spoke as little as possible to Candice, volunteering no information whatsoever. When Gull did speak she made a big show of the considerable effort she was making to communicate in English. She almost completely ignored Prity, blanking her at every opportunity.

Candice was mystified at the attitude of the disdainful Gull. From her perspective, Candice could not see how the connections she offered could in any way represent a problem, and put the matter down to some kind of misunderstanding. She was very wrong about that.

Enough interaction had taken place for Gull's team to be drawn into working with Dälight. A few lengthy planning meetings were convened, the most memorable being one that happened when Prity was out of town at some CKK get together. Candice was obliged to sit through a six–hour meeting of the HWI–Gujarat team conducted entirely in Gurjurati with no translation. Candice sat and fumed at this blatant piece of torture designed to infuriate and discourage her even more.

Dälight made arrangements for the HWI–Gujarat team to deliver training in advanced sisal–basket weaving and design, sandal making skills, forming a cooperative, financial management, and marketing. Watching how the process of planning and delivering training unfolded was an education.

Being an NGO, HWI operated according to the pattern of training that had become traditional in so many parts of the world. Those invited were offered financial compensation for their loss of earnings; travel to and from the venue, accommodation and good food while there. The budget was owned by HWI–Gujarat and Candice was required to put in a considerable wedge on behalf of Dälight. She did not need to call on CKK funds, as this first project had been built into her startup business plan.

The training was an absolute sell–out. Two weeks of seminars were convened in a rebuilt Catholic Church. People came from far and wide, banners were made, photographs taken, certificates presented, grins exchanged and of course payments made. Most of those who came expressed a desire to work together collaboratively. Candice was thrilled and even Gull's stiff back began to flex a little in all the excitement of the presentation day.

Finally, Candice felt that her work here could make a real difference. It was fantastic to be able to send back some great photographs of what she was doing, accompanied by a glowing report of the wonderful work of HWI–Gujarat.

But there was one cow pat on this otherwise flawless lawn. In the weeks that followed not one new business started up and not one cooperative came together. No–one could demonstrate a single improvement to their economic situation as a result of the programme, except for loss of earnings compensation, the bus fare and a meal. Candice resolved with Prity to look again at those values to see what may have gone wrong.

10. HOOKED

Casper had some serious thinking to do. The best place to do that, he decided, was out over the reef in his beloved Wellcraft 232 sport fishing boat. The boat was wonderfully equipped and fitted with a bomb proof 200HP Evinrude. As he admired the curvaceous symmetry of the propeller he could hear in his head the conversation he'd enjoyed with the Marine Sports Inc. salesman.

'Is it a reliable make of engine?'

'Mr. Evinrude invented the outboard motor. Keep it serviced and it will outlast the hull.'

He was very proud of the superbly sleek craft with its wonderfully powerful engine. It was his favourite toy.

Casper had decided to take his best friend Chip along to keep the mood from getting too somber. He impatiently awaited Chip's arrival at the Seaforth slipway, bridling at the slight delay. After 15 irritating minutes he saw with a wash of pleasure the familiar wide grin and excited wave of the effortlessly genial

Seeing Laodicea

Managing Director of Droneview Inc. Chip was driving his Ford truck, the gorgeous Faye by his side smiling, pleased for him to be doing what he loved. She had come to see them off.

Things had looked up for Chip since Faye came on the scene. He'd rarely been without a girl on his arm throughout their college days. They loved him almost as much as the camera did; especially when he made the football team. Handsome, hilarious, dynamic and stylish, as catches go, he was the big one — eclipsing even Casper in animal magnetism.

After a string of semi–serious relationships, Chip had been knocked off his feet by the formidable Faye. Curvy, beautiful and iron–willed she was more than a match for his rapier wit, and the one woman he couldn't outsmart in verbal banter.

They'd met up at the end of her senior spring semester, just after the presentation and defence stage of her thesis. Being a conscientious and achievement–oriented student, only once the pressure had finally lifted had she increased her social diary a little and met Chip at some debating event. Faye was a member of the Dartmouth Forensic Union at the time and had made the team for the National Debate Tournament.

At first she was uninterested in football and couldn't care less whether he played for a team or not. She most certainly did not turn into a mat for him to walk on the moment he casually divulged news of his fame. That was a first!

Daughter of a pastor, principled and well read, she was more interested in ethics than athletics. She was thrilled by the way Chip was able to light up a room and gave him feedback on what he did best. She, being a consummate public speaker and an excellent written communicator herself had improved his already significant competence and influence in public events and presentations.

Of course she became a great Big Green fan in no time at all — astounding her friends among whom she had demonstrated a lifelong disdain for ball sports. He had become a regular in the audience at debates, something which had also taken his friendship group by surprise.

They married immediately after college, moving to San Diego where he had taken the reigns of Droneview. She had been recruited by a significant nonprofit administrative software house for which she offered communications consultancy to their clients. The couple had excelled in their commercial roles, and both were committed to their local church, something Casper would not have predicted for Chip, looking back at his Dartmouth days,

Chip loved to be around her, whistled and sang on his way home from work and organised spontaneous little treats for her. He'd even learned to check her diary so that his delight for spontaneity didn't cut too catastrophically across her desire for an organised life. She, knowing his love for spontaneity was smart enough to schedule some. Friends would be briefed to "suddenly" suggest something. "Planned spontaneity" she called it. He was completely in love and she very much appreciated being discovered, and being the source of so much delight in him.

Recently Faye had presented Chip with baby Sawyer and his friend had come alive in completely new ways in response.

'She gets the best out of him as a man' thought Casper as he watched them approach. 'She's so good for him — he's living the dream.' He was thrilled for his friend, and not a little jealous. Casper had completely blown the one relationship he'd had with a woman of this kind of quality.

As their F150 glided slowly to a standstill beside him Casper returned their grins; jumping back in alarm as an enormous wolf whistle pierced the air. Chip howled with laughter jumping out of the driver's seat and folding him into a man hug. Ha! Got it fitted this morning, whaddya think?

'I think Faye might have something to say about who it gets used on!'

Seeing Laodicea

'He can use it on whoever he likes so long as they are male!'

With an exaggerated flounce and a cheery wave she was off with Sawyer to eat ice cream and throw stuff around in a ball pit.

From the Seaforth slipway the two friends sped out across the bay, anchoring just by the kelp beds off La Jolla.

After the usual banter about who would catch what, they settled into silent, pensive watchfulness. Their friendship was such that they were completely relaxed in one another's company and silence did not need to be broken. As his rod jiggled gently to the tugging of his live sand eel bait, Casper's thoughts turned to the disruption that exposure to poverty was causing his life.

Having put "boots on the ground" in a South African township he had begun to own for himself the problem that poverty was a reality destroying the lives of millions of people.

Getting people out of poverty was tougher than it might have at first appeared.

Their reasons for their being in poverty would likely be many and varied, linked to poor choices, prejudice, misfortune, disability, lack of education and opportunity as well as family income, parental survival, personal health, diet, and housing.

To take an uneducated person in poor health, living in a shack on starvation rations, depressed and with a low work ethic and transform them into a person with hope and a bright future was an almost insurmountable challenge. It would surely be easier to walk away but he couldn't; not now he was engaged.

A bite jolted Casper back to focusing on the rod, which he wound in, took a small and unexciting striped slightly mottled bass of his hook, and tossed it back into the ocean gently, watching with a small feeling of pleasure as it accelerated away from the boat, free.

He re-baited, switching to squid to see if that would attract something bigger. He winced as his selected squid curled itself around his finger and rasped its sandpaper tentacle along one of his knuckles. This always made him jump when it happened, and he adjusted the position of his hand, continuing the task with greater concentration. Once his tackle was back at the bottom; his thoughts returned to altruism.

There was something he had heard in South Africa that would not leave him. It had come from Blair on the night he'd been asked to speak at the build team's nightly worship and devotions meeting. Casper had made notes and jotted down references. He reached for his small journaling pocket book, a constant companion since he'd begun meeting intentionally with Rick and Pam.

> 'The Bible always sides with the poor. Jesus didn't just identify with the poor, he was poor. He chose to come at what he did from the angle of poverty. We're told he lived a blameless life. I guess that included avoiding any complicity in indirect crimes committed against the poor by the collective behaviour of the privileged.'

It hadn't occurred to Casper before his recent adventures that a huge amount of the privilege he'd enjoyed his whole life came about because of his indirect ability to take advantage of the poor. He was a part of a powerful collective, being an American Citizen, and was actually very proud of that. Some of the things his powerful collective did were regrettable. But maybe that was true of all powers — especially superpowers.

Blair had had more for him to chew over.

> 'Jesus' kid brother James — himself a sceptic throughout Jesus' own ministry — subsequently penned some of the most pertinent thoughts in the New Testament regarding the brevity of wealth and how it is viewed from God's eternal perspective. Through James' prophetic writing it seems like God is somehow taking a look back at the conduct of the rich from after their lives have ended.

Seeing Laodicea

'By now their flesh has decayed and their treasure has corroded. We'll pick up his words by reading from our Bibles, as James comes to pinpoint the source of their wealth. How it was that they had been able to accumulate more than their fair share.

'"...This corroded treasure you have hoarded will testify against you on the day of judgment. For listen! Hear the cries of the field workers whom you have cheated of their pay. The cries of those who harvest your fields have reached the ears of the Lord of Heaven's Armies."

'The day of judgement is simply this: the moment the poor have been waiting for. It is the inescapable event where the Righteous Judge hears the cases of the oppressed and redresses the balance of human sin and selfishness. Make no mistake my friends, that day is coming.

'I wonder if you are looking forward to it as much as the poor widow, walking on stick-thin legs; that your greed has emaciated — dressed in rags bought from wages that your low prices and wide margins have afforded. How will you feel as her toothless haggard face, wracked with the old age of her bitter 38 years of hunger, disease and hardship, looks at you; and her little bundle of possessions, makes its own case for justice to lift her up?

'What will be your thoughts as you stand in line awaiting your turn? Will a massive stinking pile of junk; rusting supercars, rotting boats, crumbling mansions, and moth-eaten Prada, stand in evidence of your greed? When the wages that were paid to the workers and farmers that sustained your lifestyle are exposed before all; how would you expect the Judge to call it? Will his just and righteous verdict lift you up or cast you down?'

Casper had probably never felt an emotion like the one that came as he'd heard these words. His mind had jumped from the little South African hall to his Dodge RAM 350 and to the Wellcraft 232 in which he now sat brooding, listening to the gentle lap of the bay's wavelets as they jostled along the port side. He had been pierced by the thought of how he had come about the money to purchase these — his two favourite toys.

Formerly a superb and secretive spread betting shark, Casper had picked up a tip from a drunken old pro that there was a huge amount of action in agrochemical options in and around the Sahel Belt of Sub-Saharan Africa. He had noticed a predictable price spike in millet and rice at certain times of the year and spotted a trend towards rising prices of the same staples year on year in major cities in the region. That kind of acuity had paid off massively, and with some of the profits, one year he'd bought his truck and boat.

Even now as he sat in one of his indulgent possessions and allowed the words to play on his mind, he knew for certain that he could not contemplate forgoing this amazing lifestyle. He could afford to be indulgent in his generosity but could he afford to allow that to impinge on his love of fishing, machines, gorgeous homes and ingenious gadgets?

It was the words of James from the New Testament that had cut through the dazzling array of distractions. James seemed to have had a complete lifestyle re-think himself at some stage in his life. Casper had taken to reading the New Testament for himself since South Africa and had noticed only that morning an extraordinary little tidbit. Jesus had appeared to James alone after his resurrection. It seems that he paid his brother a personal visit.

This transformative conversation saw James and Jesus' mother — both previously disengaged from Jesus' ministry — present at Pentecost when the Holy Spirit ignited and equipped the church. James had gone on to become a pillar of the church and indeed to write a book of the New Testament.

There was something significant in what had happened to James, who'd gone from a position of looking down at Jesus' ministry, to becoming a pillar within it. Meeting Jesus in bodily form after he'd been raised from the dead appeared to be what made the difference in James. The evidence in Scripture and the logic in

Seeing Laodicea

Casper's head made the connection easily. It was however what he couldn't see clearly that was so deeply concerning.

Casper's eyes were starting to open to the fact that he had not once considered if those funding his lifestyle were adequately paid. His mind whipped back to a conversation with one of his ex–girlfriends, Candice.

> 'And when you talk about your team, are you including the workers in your factories who build products to high standards for chicken feed? In their desperation they and their families will take a job — any job to keep from destitution and the desperate decisions of poverty; like selling bodies or children. Does it matter to you that the jobs they are offered are almost without employment rights and pay wages that in themselves perpetuate poverty?'

How that battering she'd given him came back to haunt him now! He was nailed, right there in the Bible; and no he wasn't looking forward with any relish to facing the Judge.

Casper had quite a lot of expensive kit that would stand in evidence against him — of how he had taken more than his fair share. And no, he hadn't paid his workers what their work was worth. That was a bummer. It was almost as if these words, written 2000 years ago were designed to describe the global capitalist system. The whole thing was rigged to allow the citizens of richer nations to accumulate possessions at the expense of the poor. He'd built his fortune on the benefit of these margins and spent their money on his luxuries.

Until Casper's trip to South Africa, where Blair had passed on his understanding regarding justice, nobody had explained to him how exposed everyone involved was by this Biblical text. He, more than most, was undone by its words which told his fortune — quite literally. He felt the shiver of forthcoming public humiliation; a premonition of being naked in the face of his accuser. When all respectable veneers were stripped away the motives and methods of his accumulation were indefensible. That was fine until he found himself having to make a defence.

As he flicked through his journal, one last pertinent quote came back to him from Blair; this time not from the Bible but from some New York preacher, Tim Keller. Keller maintains apparently, that greed is a sin which affects the 'spiritual eyesight' — whatever that is. It seems that it is a self–concealing problem. Those afflicted by greed find it almost unnoticeable. When the subject comes up, they find it extremely difficult to apply it to their life. In Jesus' discourses it tends to be preceded by stories about eyes and blindness. If the eye is not working — despite there being plenty of light around — the body in question walks in darkness.

Casper, illuminated and exposed by James' writing two millennia earlier, had at least had his spiritual hearing tipped off by Blair. Casper was a greedy man who had plundered the poor for his pile; and here he was off La Jolla, floating in the evidence. It felt good gently moving to the swell in idyllic surroundings, using excellent equipment; and yet it felt terrible.

Knowing you have a disease is one thing. Getting successful treatment is another. Almost before he could focus on the matter; his mind defaulted to dazzling thoughts of those who were even greedier than he. Casper, nailed and ready to be contrite, was happy to be distracted by them; but still he had no peace.

Chip's rod bucked excitingly and Casper looked on, part elated for Chip, part gutted that it was not his own rod. Chip struck, the rod arched weightily and he began to reel in. After a few moments, Chip stopped reeling. He was looking down at his hand in a puzzled uncomprehending way. He made a couple more shaky turns, then stopped again. Casper, aware from the bend on the rod that the fish was large but not overly so, called across from his seat.

'What's up buddy? You worn that wrist out somehow?' This with a sly grin.

Chip gamely returned the grin but was looking concerned and exasperated. His hand was visibly trembling a little.

Seeing Laodicea

'There's something wrong with my hand. I must have banged it on something or maybe strained it at the driving range. Can you take the rod, Cas? I can't get the reel to turn.'

He handed the tackle over, and Casper quickly continued the recovery. There was nothing wrong with the reel. The handover had not been quick enough though, and Casper viewed the slack line and felt the weightless wind–in with disappointment. Whatever had been causing the excitement was gone.

Casper returned the rod to Chip, who re–baited with exaggerated care. That was the last action of the day and both sat unspeaking; each alone with his thoughts until the lowering sun and the obvious lack of marine interest in their rigs made the decision to return straightforward. Not today the reluctant departure from the fishing grounds at the last glimmer of evening light. They were back on the slipway with plenty of daylight in which to winch the boat onto the trailer, strap it down and hose it over. Chip came with Casper as he towed it to the lockup, and joined him in the bar for an adult beverage.

'What happened back there with that fish?' Casper asked.

'I don't know; my hand went a bit tingly and I couldn't hold the reel handle properly.'

'Has it happened before?'

'No, the only thing I've had trouble with is a problem with my neck. I hurt it a few weeks back. The injury has made my arms twitch a bit but the physio says it will clear when the neck heals. Oh wait, I dropped the car keys on Monday; felt fairly similar then. Guess I'll need to get it checked out, probably nothing.'

Casper dropped his friend off, taking great care to ensure that the clothes peg which had been passing between them for around four years was fastened to the rear belt loop of Chip's trousers.

11. STONED

Benjamin sat in the bar, still shaken up and thoroughly stressed. Lamin, the bar tender carefully and skilfully rigged his hookah, ensuring the opium and tobacco mixture was properly smouldering.

The glass pipe leading from the clay chamber forced the resulting smoke to bubble its way through the glass water chamber that was cooling it. From there a rubber hose ran to the mouth piece on which Benjamin sucked deeply, slowly, vacantly.

As his eyes lidded and the corneas shrunk to pin pricks, Benjamin drifted into a hallucinogenic world of shifting shapes and colours, apparitions and dreams. Finally his pain was dulled and he could escape the constant gnawing disquiet and anxiety of his mixed economy of fraudulent empire and altruistic mission. He was an occasional but not infrequent visitor to the bar when in Serrekunda. It was tempting to be a more regular attendee but he resisted. Discretion regarding his position in society and the medical knowledge to understand the mental health risks, kept the equilibrium between the two overriding needs, to kill pain and to maintain his status, stably low.

107

Seeing Laodicea

To add to his ordinary levels of stress, Benjamin had endured an outrageous 48 hours. He needed more relief than Aminata could give him.

Benjamin had attended "God's Evangelical Church of the Gambia" in Banjul for the four years he'd owned property here. There was enough distance between Banjul and Faraja, Serrekunda where he lived for him to avoid too much contact with fellow congregants between services. Benjamin had acted as he always did, buying himself into a position of authority while avoiding any kind of accountability or personal disclosure to the church elders. They took his money and felt privileged to include him and his wallet in the leadership team. Church attendance here in the Gambia was seen as reasonably respectable and there was a certain reverence given to the pastors and leaders. However things were changing in the nation and those changes had even begun to bite Benjamin.

In Benjamin's opinion, the changes had started back in 2011 when NATO–dominated forces had facilitated the murder of Muammar Gadaffi, whose regime was an important trading partner with the Gambia.

Political tensions reached something of a peak when President Yahya Jammeh and his Armed Forces Provisional Ruling Council (AFPRC) left the British Commonwealth in 2013. Jammeh and the AFPRC had been in Government since their coup overthrew its democratically elected predecessors.

From 2013, the Gambia's relationship with the European Union had become extremely strained over issues arising from perceived human rights violations by Jammeh's regime. He had conducted 13 or more executions many of which were perceived to have been the elimination of political opponents.

Demonstrations in the streets, the burning of flags and general unrest among the people, incited by the political leadership, had created an atmosphere of further hostility towards Europeans.

Benjamin's primary relationships were with the United States which was seen as fairly neutral on account of Obama's colour and his understanding of and possible warmth towards the Islamic world. United Medical's Gambian staff team spent considerable time working with the US Embassy and Benjamin himself linked up with the UN headquarters regularly. The US and the UN were perceived as necessary friends by the government here. Much needed funding and stability for an impoverished nation came from these sources, surrounded as it was by French–speaking Senegal. If Senegal decided to cut up rough, then Gambia would need its decreasing number of friends, to survive.

Though the majority of Gambians were Moslem, of the Sunni and Sufi strain they were not particularly committed to the Koran, or warm towards embracing any kind of Sharia law. Their Islamic leaders seemed happy enough to live alongside other faiths. In many villages syncretism was the norm. In the commemorative Arch 22, created in Banjul to celebrate Jammeh's rise to power, the cosy relationships between occult–shamen practitioners, Roman Catholicism and Islam were displayed for all to see. Fallen angels found in the pages of Biblical scripture were declared "most holy" and worshipped as deities. This veneration was granted as if being mentioned in the bible legitimised spiritual status, despite such reference depicting them as enemies of God.

In recent years, in parallel with the political unrest, the behaviour of Moslems in the Gambia had become increasingly Islamist and militant. Wherever a new church was authorised a mosque would be built next door or opposite. If a Moslem became apostate by converting to another religion they could expect hostility and violence and concerted efforts to reconvert them.

In common with his near immunity to the anti–European sentiments, most of these pressures passed Benjamin by. He was far too powerfully connected to be vulnerable.

As his mind slipped into the numbing release of his opiate fix, Benjamin's battered body relaxed; limbs loose and nerveless, jaw slack. He returned to the mouth piece, again and again. Like an infant craving milk, his whole being craved release.

Seeing Laodicea

As was usual, God's Evangelical Church of the Gambia met yesterday — on Friday morning, the congregation steadily building up over the first hour. Benjamin had arrived as things properly got going.

He had been enjoying the swaying rhythmic experience, when a rumble of angry voices started to cut through the sound of the music.

The volume of shouting and chanting coming from across the road, along with the thunder of many people running had quickly grown to a roar, and the sound of damage being done to the compound wall and gates, alarmed the worshippers. Rocks began to thud into the church walls, and a window broke, showering the women in the choir with tiny shards of glass.

Pastor Edward, originally from Sierra Leone ran out into the compound to find out what was happening and spoke with the attackers. Most of the remainder of the congregation moved to the other side of the compound away from the gates, and began to pass the children and smaller women over the wall, enabling them to escape via the neighbours' premises.

A shuddering crash had announced that the gates were no more and an angry mob of Moslem men surged into the compound, some holding sticks and bottles.

The remainder of the congregation ran frantically to the staircase at the far end of the church and while the women rushed upstairs, the men, including Benjamin, gathered around the door to the small stairwell. Here they took a terrible beating as one by one they slipped through the door behind their decreasing little knot of unarmed defenders. Benjamin was one of the first to squeeze through the door and waited with the others as each of the church's men struggled through the doorway to join them. Miraculously everyone made it, mainly because the mob in its fury and disorganised violence had obstructed itself in its mission to tear them apart.

110

With everyone somehow through the doorway the men held the door shut behind them as though their lives depended upon it, which of course they did. Meanwhile, the women upstairs were subjected to a volley of rocks with which the mob pelted their windows. Flying glass and stones whizzed among the women, ripping flesh and drawing whimpers and cries of pain from them. There were three beds in the rooms upstairs and those trapped there built a little barricade of the mattresses, huddling behind to avoid the worst of the barrage.

In the church, frustrated by their inability to get at the hated Christians, the mob began to tear the place apart.

Upstairs, the women called the police station. Their panic stricken call was met with an unperturbed flat monotone from the policeman who picked up. It was Friday — there were no officers available to be dispatched, they were all at prayers.

The women then called the army barracks and received a similar message. The church was left helpless, abandoned to the fury of the mob that had come from the mosque.

Downstairs the congregation's men listened in horror through the door as they heard their place of worship being vandalised. They cried out in anguish, calling on God for intervention. They were mostly very poor people whose gifts to the church had been a significant sacrifice. What was happening in the church was painful to their ears, and somehow not being able to see, cowering in fear behind the door amplified the sounds.

After a very long ten minutes or so, the attackers seemed, to the cowering, fearful Christians, to have lost interest and all went quiet as the Moslems had fled the scene, almost guiltily.

The sudden peace drew the Churchgoers out of their hiding place. Nervous, fearful and shaken, they regarded the destruction. They found an unscathed Pastor Edward who stood among bits of splintered furniture, shredded fabric, loose masonry and shards of glass. Some of the women started drifting down the stairs, wailing with relief at the sight of all the men still alive. The people then began tending to the wounded. Broken limbs and fractured heads, ripped eyes and lumps and bumps abounded. Benjamin had escaped serious injury but found a big lesion on his shin. He'd also received a split lip. His hair had been pulled and his knuckles were swollen and grazed from where the door had slammed shut on his hand.

Being medically trained, he'd been able to conduct a makeshift triage using a quickly repaired table, with his medical bag and first aid kit from the car, some ripped shirts and bowls of water. He tacked together a couple of gaping wounds and probably saved one young woman's life by stabilising a ripped artery.

Pastor Edward had the congregation in a brief prayer and dismissed the church to their homes. Those with vehicles took the most injured to hospital.

At 4 p.m. the same afternoon, the church leaders gathered and discussed what had happened.

Pastor Edward explained events to the others from his perspective.

He had run to meet the mob just as they had come through the destroyed gate. He had held up his hands and shouted to stop them. The angry crowd had flowed around him without touching him and gone through to attack his people. He had found himself at the back of the mob uninjured, shocked and extremely shaken. There he discovered the Imam and some other clerics calmly overseeing the attack. They had been surprised to see him and more than a little embarrassed. He had demanded that they get their people under control. At first they had claimed they had followed the crowd down in order to try and restrain things, and had been unable to do anything to stop the attack.

Pastor Edward, filled with fury and righteous indignation, would not be brushed aside. In the face of his authoritative leadership, the moral imperative of the mosque's leaders had won the day. Within a few minutes they had not been able to withstand the Pastor's insistence that they intervene any longer. The Imam himself had issued instructions to withdraw, and the crowd had melted away almost immediately.

The leaders had given thanks to God for the fact that the children had escaped, that Edward had been spared, that the Imam had listened to reason and that there had been no loss of life.

The church leaders, standing in the wreckage of their place of worship, then called the mosque and spoke with a cleric, asking for an explanation regarding what had happened. The man, Mamadu, had promised to call back.

He did so a few minutes later and said that the leaders of the mosque regretted that the attack had happened assuring the church that Islam was a religion of peace. He was very keen that the two communities were reconciled and stated that he along with other Moslem leaders would like to meet at the church at 6 p.m. for initial talks.

The church leaders were pleased that there was such a swift and positive response from the mosque leaders. They prayed together for the injured and asked for peace, then disbursed to take some food. They made their way back to the church premises at 5:30 to assess the damage and ready themselves for the conversation with the Imams.

At 6:30 there was no sign of the Islamic leaders so the church men decided to begin the clear-up.

All of the chairs were broken, but cannibalising the more seriously smashed casualties allowed them to save two thirds. Most were only smashed apart rather than having had struts or legs broken, and slotted back together OK. The church had not suffered any fire damage which was a blessing. It had however lost its PA kit, all musical instruments, Bibles, pulpit, fixtures and fittings. The building had been stripped, many items ripped from the plaster. Only belongings that were inaccessible, hidden or too strongly attached had survived.

Seeing Laodicea

At 7 p.m. just as darkness fell, the sounds of heavy vehicles were heard. The men had stepped outside and watched with astonishment the approach of an armoured car and two large military lorries; carrying around ten soldiers in uniform.

The officer in charge jumped down from the truck. He announced that they were all under arrest for inciting a riot. The Christians offered no resistance and, bewildered, allowed themselves to be shoved into one of the lorries.

Just before being loaded into the truck, Edward managed to fire off a hurried text to his wife alerting her of his arrest. He was unable to tell her where they were being taken; he assumed it was to the army barracks. His phone, along with all the others was removed minutes later by an aggressive and unpleasant soldier.

In fact they were taken a considerable distance to Brikama police station along the South Bank road, well clear of the combos (the area around the Atlantic coast and the capital).

They carefully but hurriedly negotiated the dizzyingly long drop down from the back of the lorry to the road. There had been time on the journey to process what had happened. They all felt very uneasy, most had been silent.

Benjamin, easily the most authoritative, commandingly vociferous and indignant of the captives, demanded to speak to the UN chief of staff whom he knew by name. The soldier responsible for escorting him responded, in heavily accented English, rich with the deep tones of West Africa.

'I have no idea to whom you are referring, foreigner.'

Benjamin, rattled, tried another tack.

'Do you know who I am?'

'No foreigner, I do not. Do you know who I am?'

'No of course I do not.'

114

'Then you do not know who did this!'

With that the soldier crunched his rifle into Benjamin's groin. Benjamin sank to the ground gasping as pain exploded in his lower abdomen. He was down on all fours for some time before he could recover himself sufficiently enough to struggle back to his feet.

Cruel, harsh laughter broke out among the soldiers. Benjamin's brutal captor was thumped between the shoulder blades by an appreciative colleague. The grinning, sneering soldiers then proceeded to hand responsibility for the prisoners to the police offers in charge of the station, before roaring off in the trucks.

When the guards finally left them alone, the six prisoners stood for a while, then sat one by one.

After a while, Edward rose to his feet and raised his voice.

'My brothers we have a choice to make. We can either sit in the dirt with heavy anxious hearts, or we can visit Heaven. Which will it be?'

As the men sang and worshipped God, Benjamin experienced transcendence beyond any experience he'd ever had. What followed was a strengthening, heartening, life–giving presence entered the cells. It was a moment which caused the men to wish their time together would be extended rather than shortened.

The police guards provided water but no food. In the heat of the night the prisoners were glad of the drink and unaware of their hunger.

When finally it came time to sleep, they had curled up on the floor, each having used the bucket. At first, the act of using the latrine bucket one at a time while being watched by the others, caused the men to approach the function ashamedly. Things were awkward until a ribald good humour set in and the competitive spirit of men turned the activity into something of a game.

Seeing Laodicea

Injured, incarcerated, dirty, deprived of comfort; comrades in adversity, they were glad to be together. Even Benjamin who had never experienced such close fellowship with brothers before felt strangely good about what was happening. Momentarily, he was not alone.

Edward's wife Fanta contacted the army by telephone, where she was met with a stone wall. No information was forthcoming. She knew that to present herself at the barracks was to risk gang rape. She was distraught, losing her mind with worry. She gathered the other wives and church members to pray and they spent the night making calls to the police and the army. Of course, they prayed.

Nobody in authority was available to answer their requests for information. One young lad called Kebba, son of Nfansu, the oldest of those arrested, went to the army barracks. He was not granted admittance, was given no information and escaped a beating only by virtue of his speed and agility when he pressed the guard at the gate too hard.

The women had to go about their daily routines. The children had needed their attention as usual, and most mothers had incomes to earn. Life, even in the Combos was extremely tough and every dalasi was hard to come by. For these women life had been put on hold, and yet because the demands of life as a mother and breadwinner continue unabated, it also hadn't been on hold at all.

In the market place, a friend of Aminata overheard a conversation between two Fulani women at the stall where she sold fish. One of the women she heard was a cleaner in the barracks at Banjul.

Aminata's friend heard the cleaner telling her companion that a soldier on duty that morning was furious that a group of political prisoners arrested in Banjul had needed to be transported all the way over to Brikama the previous evening, to be held in custody. He had missed out on an important liaison with a particularly

116

exciting young lady as a result of spending half the night taking pastors on an outing.

Aminata called Fanta, who in turn contacted the Malian embassy, informing them that their citizen, Benjamin Traoré was being held illegally by the Gambian government in Brikama police station.

There was a terrible commotion at Brikama police station around midday on Saturday. A big, aggressive and extremely authoritative voice had entered the premises demanding in English, to see the officer in charge. Shouting on arrival was unusual. To yell at a police officer inside a police station was to invite a beating — everybody knew that.

The desk officer, typically demonstrative in his passivity and disinterest, first registered mild surprise, which quickly turned to anger. He did not remove his boots from the desk, nor did he look the fool at the counter in the eye.

'I am in charge here and if you are here to speak with me you should lower your voice.'

There was menace in his tone. A man in command of his surroundings, quietly relaxed, bone idle; the police officer had perfected the art of only standing when he could not sit, and sitting when he could not lie down, for years. His body displayed the attributes of a busted sofa. No matter what you covered it with, it would always look scruffy.

He pursed his lips and sucked in his breath, exuding self–importance. He decided to make his visitor suffer for the tone he'd used. He guessed this man was a pastor and was going to demand the release of the prisoners. Well one more broken head in a cell would do no harm.

It was however the visitor who filled the conversational space the policeman's pregnant, expressive pause created, by speaking first.

Seeing Laodicea

'On your feet you Wolof dog if you want to keep that uniform one more day!'

The officer involuntarily snapped to his feet, the military officer tone of this command was absolutely irresistible and he obeyed before he thought about it.

Having now looked properly at his visitor, the officer's persona quickly registered alarm. This was not a military man, but he was a very powerful one. The officer's eyes flicked to the large white 4x4 outside the station, the uniformed chauffeur at the wheel, and the diplomatic flag fluttering above the bonnet.

'I understand that you are holding one of my citizens against his will, having illegally arrested him yesterday. Explain yourself!'

'I don't understand boss, we have only some rioters from a Christian demonstration in custody.' Whining and truly worried, the desk sergeant was over his pay scale.

'Nonsense! I want the name of the person responsible — get me the Attorney General on the telephone now!'

'I cannot do that boss.'

'Then I demand to be arrested. You will then have two ministers to call; both him and my friend Bakari — the Minister for Foreign Affairs. If you will not arrest me I will assault you and smash up your office until you are forced to arrest me!'

The desk sergeant had made the call.

As soon as he got through to the Minister, the Consul was over the counter, and all over him.

'Give me that phone!'

The sergeant meekly handed it over. The volume of the call had been so loud that the prisoners in the cells could clearly hear everything going on.

'Abdou, is that you? Yes, it is Consul Souéloum Diagho here of the Malian Consulate to the Gambia. I am in your cattle shed of a police station in Brikama, where you have had the audacity to lock up my friend Benjamin Traoré. I demand an explanation.'

There was a silence while the requisite explanation was made.

'Abdou, that is not an explanation. That is disgraceful shambling waffle. It is nonsense and I expect to see you over here in Brikama to make a personal apology to me and to Benjamin as soon as you can get here. I am waiting for your car to come.'

Another lengthy silence had followed. The prisoners in the cells listened wonderingly.

'You have not understood me Minister.'

Souéloum Diagho had been shouting at a level that must surely have distorted the signal. He had also dispensed with the first name protocol.

'If you do not do what I say, I will arrange to be arrested and the next call you receive will be from my government's Minister of Foreign Affairs, who is likely to declare diplomatic war at my request. If that happens, the trading friends of Mali — which of course include Senegal — will begin to regard your tiny little strip of land as an unacceptable credit risk.

'You will then have to pay double the price for food imports and will lose your credit agreements. If you really upset us, we will ask our good friends, the Senegal Government, to swallow you up and divide your territory between us. Then you will need to learn to speak French. I do not care that you have an important family engagement, I have just cancelled it. Now get over here and make your apologies.'

A truly angry Consul is a formidable foe. Diagho was not finished yet. He slammed down the telephone and went for the now terrified desk sergeant.

Seeing Laodicea

'Take me through to the cell where you have Benjamin, and lock me in. Then call the Attorney General back and tell him where I am and that I will not come out until he makes his formal apology to both of us in person. In the meantime we will need lunch. Go and get enough goat meat and tapalapa for all the prisoners being held with me. Now move!'

The Attorney General did not appear to make the apology in person but sent an official pardon. All the prisoners received their lunch and were transported home by limousine and police car.

For Benjamin, there was a lot to process. His first genuine experience of the God he'd nominally worshipped all his life had come in a prison cell. That experience had been as the result of terrifying and injurious persecution.

But, here in Lamin's bar, rather than reflecting on his experiences with a view to making some spiritually developmental progress, Benjamin was defaulting to the only course of action he could cope with. He was getting stoned.

12. CHEERS

There came an excited squeal from Candice's mom as her daughter emerged from baggage reclaim at Lindbergh Field airport, San Diego.

It had been a full six months since she had last seen her daughter, during which time she had been a daily visitor to the State Department's India section and also to timesofindia.com website scanning always for threats to Americans. She had worried herself into quite a mess at first but after a few months had become accustomed to the nagging fears. Now she saw Candice again, her emotions overwhelmed her.

Candice disentangled herself, allowed mom to wheel her larger bag, and hurried through the exit to shift the car before the parking charges mounted more than was necessary.

From the airport, they headed straight for In–n–Out Burger, opting for the drive through. Candice had been on curry and chapattis for months, with occasional bouts of sickness, consequently losing six pounds in weight. She felt entitled to a "double double" with animal style fries. She had endured years of strict training regimes, so burgers were not part of the plan. Also, her mom had been on a single mom budget for most of Candice's formative years so a trip to In-n-Out, was something reserved for a celebration occasion, usually after some success. Both women felt deliciously guilty sinking their teeth into their carbs and fat binge. Candice enjoyed the sweetness of the condiments, but apart from the pickle and onion in her burger found the taste very bland.

The journey from India, via Istanbul had been a long one, totalling 34 hours including bus rides and connection delays. Bone tired, her own bed was a delight and Candice slept for twelve hours straight.

Late November was the perfect season to time her return. Thanksgiving had dragged most of her friends back to San Diego to spend time with their families. It was also football season and being a previous athletics team member as a flying cheerleader, Candice had free entry to Aztecs games. She went for a wonderful night out to watch them take on Hawaii.

Seeing a game from the stands was a strange experience for Candice. The vast number of players trotting around before kick off, resplendent in their mainly black kit with flame red flashes made an impressive spectacle. The cheerleader and marching band displays had her twitching as she watched the footwork with an expert eye, appreciating the many hours of practice that lay behind these performances.

Hawaii, all in white, pushed the Aztecs hard but SDSU brought home an excellent win and got their season back on track. Candice yelled and cheered, and found herself up on her feet going through some of the old moves as the girls among the crowd behind the home bench did their display in the stand.

It was a superb night out with her girl friends and she returned home dizzy with excitement and nostalgia. Despite the enjoyment of it all, the razzmatazz and good times on offer melted away like cotton candy. There was nothing here for her now, just a fun night out. All those years of striving to make the cheerleading team — the sleepless nights before games going through the moves in her head — all were worthless to her now; a fleeting moment of history forgotten by all.

Candice's main reason for being home was to meet her funders, check in with Lifted Sister, and hook up with Bella from Deaf Cat to set up the Living Dälights nonprofit online trading company.

It was great to be back in Ablaze Church and warmly welcomed to the Sunday service. She stood in her row, hands aloft slightly self-consciously. In India it would seem disengaged to not worship God with her body as well as her voice in a church service.

Here in San Diego, people were a little more reserved. In fact anyone making a spectacle of themselves unless they were on stage, where holding up one arm towards Heaven was commonplace, was seen as exhibitionist. Candice supposed that how people expressed themselves to one another was very much subjective to local culture; but to God? Well surely if she came to church primarily to express honour and love to him, how that came over to someone else might be rather more revealing of their character than hers.

Candice was introduced to the congregation, which had pretty much doubled in the two and a half years she'd been away. They hadn't completely forgotten her though. As she made her way to the front she was given a cheerleader's greeting. A line of girls with pompoms formed at the front, shaking them energetically and chanting to the same rhythm as 'SDSU' yelling 'CAN–DICE–TAY–LOR' followed by a couple of shimmies and 'LIF–TED–SIS–BOOM–BAH!'

Candice wept.

She showed a short, inexpertly iPhone–filmed montage of video clips, cobbled together into a Prezzi by Bella the night before. Rick and Pamela publicly prayed for Candice's work giving thanks for progress to date and asking for a fruitful time back in the USA.

After the service she was invited out for dinner by Casper and found herself somewhat reluctantly back at the Blue Wave, hoping desperately that it would not be a reprise of their last visit. In a way, it was kinda nice to be asked and she didn't quite have enough will power to resist.

If there was one meal other than an In–n–Out Burger that she had been craving for a while, it was a Blue Wave fish taco. Candice told herself that was the main reason she was here. This lovely man had hurt her very deeply — cruelly even — last time they sat here, when he'd dumped her in some immature tantrum. He'd followed that up with dating a string of clothes horses and hardly looking back as he tore up the town like some testosterone–charged tornado. If there's one thing that closes off a relationship with a girl like Candice, it's getting over her within 24 hours of dumping her.

Now for some inexplicable reason, he and the promised taco had combined to lure her back for more.

After a few minutes of chit–chat about football, her presentation that morning, how her mom was doing and whether his dad was still playing the field with braid–digging young female naval officers, they got down to some serious talking.

'Candice, you're looking fantastic.'

Here we go, she thought. Most men thought she looked fantastic. She prepared herself for the usual bull.

'It wasn't because of how you look that made me ask you here. I kinda need to put some stuff right OK. Don't take this the wrong way, but um I regret what happened between us.' Oh that was good; she was nice and enjoyable but regrettable.

Then the bombshell,

'I don't regret that things ended, not at all — well I regret how they ended maybe. It's triggered a lot of good things for me, got me reconsidering. What I really regret is how things between us started. I wish I could go back and do it all again properly. ...Girl like you deserves more than a fool like me.'

'Cas, I don't really understand what you're saying,' she frowned.

Casper tried to clarify some stuff he'd been musing on for nearly two and a half years.

'When you came back from Mexico and went for me over justice and human rights and all that, you started challenging my personal values. Well nobody has ever talked to me like that, not ever. It scared the heck out of me. There's some things I never told you about, things that cheapen me, make me feel pathetic and unlovable. I can't have anyone messing around on the inside of me like you did. You just freaked me out.'

Candice caught her breath. She just had him as a jackass jock that used his genitals for thinking and rode through life on a bucking ego, keeping one jump out of trouble only by his stunning IQ.

'Feelings and Casper... now there's a concept that hadn't occurred to me.' She smiled inwardly. 'If only I'd known I might have fallen for him!'

'Cas, I regret how I seduced you. It takes two to tango. You have nothing to apologise to me for. I kicked things off with you, for shallow selfish cheap reasons. The difference now is; I've connected with what I'm really about, and that just isn't chasing exciting men. I got what I deserved. Didn't like the way it ended either to be honest but I'm over you.'

Casper looked in her eyes. No tears, just the implacable thoughtful level gaze of a woman of quality, a princess of royal line. She was gone; really truly over him. He had one last thing to do.

'Candice, would you please consider something? I want to tell you some things first so you get the context.'

'OK Casper, shoot — I'll hear you out.'

'Since we broke up I got to watching how you kicked on with this new direction in your life. To be honest I couldn't — still can't —

see what's driving you. I liked what I saw though, liked it a lot. And the questions you put to me, they rocked my world. I was a success till you redefined success for me.

'I followed you round to Rick and Pamela's and found there was a way forward that I hadn't seen before. I got rid of some of the worst stuff I was struggling with too. I'm going OK now, starting to feel good about myself.

'Then, can you believe, I followed you onto one of those house building trips, only I went to South Africa, I mean, I gotta have some originality don't I?'

Candice smiled at that, he did seem to have followed the first part of her path to spiritual awakening quite closely.

'Anyways I'm determined to walk away from some of the crazy buck–chasing power trip stuff and get into social justice in a big way. Things are gonna change from now on in — some big changes coming up for me.'

Candice smiled, very encouraged by this talented man showing every sign of true spiritual development.

'So I wondered if you'd give me a chance to start over again with you. Take you out, look after you. No gymnastics or anything just dating and doing things properly.'

He wasn't speaking too clearly. Candice had heard other guys choke a bit asking her out. Her physical presence was such that men often wanted her so desperately that their emotions ran a little wild when they made a try for her. Casper had never sounded or looked like this in the past. She was actually quite touched.

'Casper, I don't want to mess you around and give you any kind of hope that things can work between us. You hurt me real bad when we broke up, and I didn't appreciate the way you ran around with stacks of women after that. I can forgive you for it of course, and maybe you can change — but neither of us can rewrite history. I am truly over you. I guess I'm even over a reformed you. My life has true meaning now. I have seen the Kingdom of God and everything else looks a bit shabby in comparison.

'You should see it Cas, in fact I think you're beginning to. It's full of courage and acts of kindness. It is a Kingdom populated by lovers, each of whom finds the object of their affection precious. They love with the kind of love that wants nothing back. More than that — it's a "place" where the King himself walks. He really does, right among us. I've seen evidence of him healing people, watched their faces when they realise he's touched them and that their body works again. When the pain and the fear and the hopelessness fall off them; it's brilliant Cas, there's truly nothing like it.'

Casper's mind went back to his observation of the girl being supernaturally healed in South Africa. He'd seen it too, but only as an outside observer. Candice sounded like she was closer to the action.

'There's more — I've already seen community transformation in Vietnam; the struggle to bring a neighbourhood from despair to flourishing. That was someone else's work. But I have a vision for more of the same flowing from my own life. I want to see people who have been crushed and downtrodden all their lives come into an opportunity to thrive. I want to see the rich and powerful think twice before they tread on my friends. I want to see people get money and want to share it because they understand how dangerous it is to desire it more than relationships.

'I look forward to the day when my friends in India can send their children to decent schools, and when they can afford medical treatment. There are so many lives I want to touch and transform that throwing myself into a relationship with one man seems, well a bit of a sell-out.'

Casper knew what was coming, he steeled himself.

Seeing Laodicea

'Thanks, Casper for a lovely meal, and I'm thrilled with where you're at. I can't date you, lovely man; I want more than you can give me. I am in search of the Kingdom of God and I know now that I will see it if I hold my ground against injustice and keep walking forward — obeying quickly what I believe God is saying.

'I have friends who want God like you would not believe. They have shown me that you can have as much of him as you want. You just have to want him more than anything — in their case, even life itself.'

So that was it then. He was out of luck.

'I get it Candice, and I love the way you're heading. I don't resent you turning me down. I'm disappointed and all, but things could be worse. Seems to me I've been up against the King of Kings and I guess that's pretty tough competition.

'One thing though girl, I will support what you're doing. If you won't become my life partner, perhaps we can be partners in another way — if you think I can handle it without going all soft on you all the time. I have heard you say no, and the matter of dating is pretty much closed unless you reopen it.'

They spent the next hour discussing her journey so far and her plans for Transparent Trade, something she had shared with no-one before. He was skeptical at first, became increasingly intrigued, then excited.

Casper called the sommelier and ordered a ludicrously expensive Cava to toast the conception of their initiative.

'Cheers!' Casper was truly excited to celebrate a fabulous and unique idea, and to potentially share its future with this lovely girl.

Candice left the table having gained a business partner whose personal wealth and track record for launching successful enterprises was pretty unmatched for his age group. She had the feeling that Transparent Trade would fly. It had been well worth coming. She also felt strangely good about herself, like she'd had closure on something.

Casper was a very smart boy indeed. He knew that Candice was unlikely to want to get things on between them again. He did though want to undo some of the damage he so regretted doing. Despite holding some small hope of wooing her back he had planned to give her the opportunity to reject him and that for two reasons.

First he had wanted to test his own resolve in growing more emotionally mature. He had passed the test he had set himself; he had allowed himself to be rejected.

Second he knew that he had hurt her and crushed her beautiful hopeful spirit when he had reacted so badly last time around. Long conversations with Rick had clarified what he had done to wound her, and he owed so much of his epiphany to her. He smiled cheerfully to himself as he strode manfully back to his apartment alone; chin up, shoulders back, feeling good. He'd made good on a lot of the damage he'd previously done to himself, shifted a shed load of guilt.

Seeing Laodicea

13. LOCKED IN

For a Monday, Casper was in good spirits, beat-boxing gently under his breath, as he went about reviewing reports. He felt sharp. The weekend had exceeded expectations, God was in his Heaven and all was right with the world: Browning, he believed.

He had already made initial enquiries about setting up a nonprofit arm to CaMPuS and his secretarial team was busily making appointments and filling out forms. Making things happen was what Casper did. It was what brought him alive. The buzz about him when something entirely fresh and exciting needed to be set in motion was infectious. His immediate team was enthusiastic and he'd called a board meeting for this afternoon to get the leadership on side. One of the drawbacks to growth was the need to share ownership.

CaMPuS Solutions Inc. was a substantial company now, very vigorous with upwards of 25 high-tech projects in development falling into three main divisions. In the long term, each project would become a listed company in its own right within an ever-burgeoning CaMPuS group. The company worked on defensive weapons systems. Given the chance, who wouldn't in San Diego

— home of the US Navy Pacific Fleet? Marine technology spin-offs into the luxury yacht market were a natural extension of the highly lucrative military wing. Once the Research and Development had been funded by the US Navy purse, slimmer non-military grade versions of his products could easily be developed.

There was one final area of development for CaMPuS that was highly secretive and kept under wraps. Military targeting mini drones. When linked to USAF offensive units these tiny aircraft are entirely dispensable and give pilots "eyes on the ground" for laser guided ordinance. Where in the past, Special Forces had been needed to put laser tags on specific targets, large reconnaissance drones could drop off Casper's tiny military grade Droneview-style craft.

The pilots are able to get right in close, flying alongside cars, or right up to buildings, giving eyes — signals relayed via the recon drones — to specialist pilots safely on US held land. Once their laser beam locks on a target, laser guided rockets or bombs can be used to destroy it in a precise surgical strike.

The decrease in collateral damage following the deployment of CaMPuS's incredible little devices was highly beneficial, and it troubled his conscience not one bit to be involved in offensive military ordinance rather than defensive.

Human shields were a nightmare for US forces, a problem that needed solving. The way Casper saw things, it should be a moral imperative that armed forces stay away from civilians. It seemed to him as though many terrorist units were now more than happy to mingle with the innocent and uninvolved — or worse — to forcibly recruit human shields. Under those circumstances Casper saw no alternative but to blast both the target and the shield and to place the responsibility squarely onto those who were evil enough to bring war to the innocent.

It did seem important, though, to improve the accuracy of delivering strikes, thus reducing the need for oversized explosions thanks to careful targeting. Casper was pleased with progress on his munitions resistant mini drone, which was already highly effectively deployed.

As with the original Droneview models, he had secured and linked multiple patents in order to increase the value of his product. Casper had combined the four–route superconductor system for flight controls, giving durability under fire. Similar to the multi–system approach taken by the Fairchild A10 tank–buster aircraft, if his drones were hit and a control line severed, another line would automatically switch in.

Casper's unique approach was to use proportionally wide swathes of the drone's skin as superconducting "wiring". The radar unobservable air frame, the anti–shake camera and the self–stabilising anti–shake mount, for laser targeting equipment supplied by the military were also linked patents. It was a brilliant piece of kit, set to send the company's value stratospheric, and which in fact it was already doing.

All progress on this product relied on the work of his genius friend Marcus Postlethwaite, who was overdue a Pizza Hut lunch — his favourite. Casper smiled as he thought of his great friend, now a fully grown lab–coat wearing, wild haired mad professor type. A creature of habit with a unique restless mind; whose ability to run through permutations and reach for little–known formulae and algorithms in conversation about non–scientific subjects always amused him. Last time they met, Marcus had been able to accurately predict how long it would take a computer to run through all possible word matches at current processor rates in a Scrabble game. He had predicted that within a year it would be possible to play Scrabble against a household computer without the game lasting inappropriately long.

He was just thinking of calling Marcus and preparing his arteries for a pizza assault, when Faye Goldstein dropped into his office near lunch time.

Faye had just come from the hospital having dropped Chip at his nearby office. She had news of tests and wanted a chat with someone she could trust.

Seeing Laodicea

Casper sat her down and fixed her a chai tea from the Keurig. It had been four months since the fishing trip where Chip had needed help with the reel. Casper had followed the progress of consultations and tests with mild but unconcerned interest. It was likely to be some sports injury, a bit of nerve damage or something that a bit of physio and rest would put right. Casper heard that arthritis could strike quite young and could be nasty, so was hoping there was nothing severe like that going on.

He saw Chip from time to time and noticed his walking was more careful. He frequently dropped things, and Faye tended to pick him up from work because his stiff neck made looking over his shoulder at angled junctions awkward.

'He's got ALS Cas.'

Casper didn't know a great deal about ALS except that a load of ice and water had been chucked about over the summer — "the ice bucket challenge". He'd made a donation himself rather than ruin his suit. In September a bunch of his employees had stood under a crane bucket at the construction site across the road. They had made an amazing video for Facebook of the event and the company put a big slice towards the charity behind the campaign. Apart from that, Casper had just caught enough of the information backwash to know it was something pretty serious.

He reached for his Mac and tapped ALS into Wikipedia. He read aloud:

> Amyotrophic Lateral Sclerosis (ALS) is a neurodegenerative disorder with various causes. ALS is characterised by muscle spasticity, rapidly progressive weakness due to muscle wasting. This results in difficulty speaking, swallowing, and breathing. ALS is the most common of the five motor neurone disorders.

This looked real bad, he glanced at Faye who sat in shocked silence, waiting for more. He paused.

'Faye, this doesn't look good. He's picked up something really uncomfortable there. What did the consultant say?'

'Well not much; I wrote down most of it. He has confirmed SOD–1 variant ALS. He will need considerable palliative care.'

As she spoke, Casper's eyes flicked to Wiki's next paragraph. He could not read this to her, not without Chip present. This was something they would have to process together. He absorbed the information silently.

Average survival time from onset to death is 39 months…

He shut the laptop immediately.

'How long has he had symptoms Faye?'

Casper kept his voice offhand, curious, neutral.

'Oh I guess about a year, looking back. He first had a bit of trembling in his arms last Christmas, then that awful neck pain that the physio was working on through spring. He started dropping things in May and when he had that trouble with the fishing reel in July he knew he ought to have it looked at.

'The physio was confident he could sort out the neck pain, so we persisted with him for another month, but Chip was dropping more things and starting to twitch more in public. We went back to the health centre in September. They thought it might be diet related at first, then possibly ME or MS. Finally, today they were able to confirm things. We felt quite relieved actually; at least we can start treatment.'

Casper did the math; 39 minus 12. So Chip more than likely had about two years, and judging by that first Wiki definition they would be awful. He could see that she was in denial or too anxious to think straight. 'Palliative; that's not treatment, it's care,' he thought.

'Where's Sawyer?' asked Casper; changing the subject.

Seeing Laodicea

'He's with Pops hanging out down at the park. I'm picking him up at 1 p.m.'

'Hey it's 12:20 already! You'd best be moving then! I'll give you a call later this evening. In the meantime why don't you and Chip have a check online together, see what you're looking at.'

She drank up her chai and was gone in a few moments, leaving a perfumed trail of loveliness behind. Casper went straight back to the Mac the moment she left the building. This was bad for Chip, real bad.

He called Chip that evening after dinner, carefully feeling for where his friend was at.

'Did you look up ALS online buddy?'

'Sure did Cas, it's not good dude!' His voice sounded flat, distant. He was making a brave effort to sound normal, but this was his best friend. Casper knew he was shaken.

'I know Chip, I had a look myself and I'm real worried for you both. What do you want me to do? Shall I come over or would you rather be alone?'

'I think we need a little space thanks friend. I'll drop by tomorrow and we can have a chat.'

After the line went dead, Casper poured himself a Jack Daniels and started surfing the web. He just caught himself absent-mindedly drifting towards some soft porn. 'Man, when I am I gonna learn not to reach for unhelpful comforts?' He chastised himself, disappointed but relieved he'd summoned the strength to avoid his old addiction.

He looked for something more wholesomely distracting — anything to keep his mind occupied. Having enjoyed the social justice conference a couple of years back, he Googled "social justice conference" and was drawn to something in L.A. in December, entitled "Do They Know It's Christmas?" named after a charity record produced in the UK in 1984. It had sold 2.5 million copies in the USA apparently, but Casper had never heard of it. He was too young.

He glanced at the list of speakers, recognising a couple; Claybourne and Campolo were there, and Blair's wife Leona from the house builders was on the team sheet. He also noticed a fellow by the name of Sir Ralph Jefferson from Light to Africa. HWI were also there. He called up Candice. Yes, she would be delighted to get a ride over there in his Porsche. He bought the tickets immediately and emailed copies to her.

Still extremely anxious and energised, sleep an impossibility, he did a little more research into agricultural issues in Sub-Saharan Africa. A group called the Alliance for a Green Revolution in Africa (AGRA) had been formed in 2008, facilitated by wealthy altruistic Americans.

AGRA had identified the need for far better efficiency in managing soil, irrigation and seed systems. Analysis of the current situation concluded that crop yields would need to double to match the 50% growth in population expected by 2025, Ebola permitting.

Now Casper was very familiar with the work of AGRA as they, among others, had been investing in the much lauded agriculture-led economic growth in Sub-Saharan Africa. It was this very thrust which had destabilised things for farmers in South Sudan, Burkina Faso and Mali. The enormous push for efficiency had seen many subsistence farmers driven from their land.

Cash cropping for the benefit of European and Middle Eastern markets had improved the balance sheet of the countries involved. Agricultural efficiency gain was certainly resulting in an excellent balance of trade improvement.

It had also triggered a cash grab among the powerful and a nightmare of land loss, staples shortage with attendant price spikes, poverty and starvation among the poor. This was the source of much of Casper's spread betting wealth. He read the announcements of the Addis Ababa Green Revolution Forum in

Seeing Laodicea

September 2014 with a genuine list of concerns for those whose voices were not being heard.

Conversations with Joseph, Eve, and Benjamin had convinced him that the powerful expatriate experts with their high–tech, high yield solutions rode rough shod over the poor. There was another story of misery playing out in the unseen sub–stratum of the powerless. The high numbers of people involved were certainly mentioned as statistics but their current needs through the revolutionary changes and their land rights did not feature highly in the conversation.

Casper did one final piece of research. In preparation for a crucial board meeting coming up at CaMPuS, he researched flight routes to Africa. Eventually he hit on Turkish Airlines from LAX into Istanbul, connecting to Ouagadougou. He could not believe the low cost, or the overall flight time. His big stack of Star Alliance points, earned mainly on American of course, meant gold card status access to lounges all the way. He made notes for his secretary and finally turned in, his head full of statistics and disruption plans. His sleep was deep and full of crazy dreams.

The following lunchtime he picked up Chip and took him to Fuddruckers for an outrageous burger fest. This was an absolute favourite for both of them. They stepped onto the checkerboard floor, grinning at the ridiculously groaning salad cart, before selecting several pounds of beef sandwiched with everything in the refrigerator into a delicious home–made bun.

Real American man food does something to a guy. They wished they'd turned up on a Harley Davidson.

Casper had immediately picked up on Chip's visible decline since the last time he'd seen him, about a month ago. He was finding it awkward to use his left hand and positioned it carefully in his lap, fingers slightly curled up. His right appeared fine and he just got on with his meal.

'Hey Chip, what's happening with your other hand?'

Casper glanced down meaningfully.

'It's been like this for a few days now. Funny really because to start with it was my right that gave me more problems.'

Casper enjoyed Chip's company and avoided talk of the disease until they had finished eating. He couldn't help noticing little differences and adaptations in his friend's approach to a simple meal since they'd last sat here in the early autumn.

Chip positioned his Coke carefully with the one good hand, leaning forward to drink from the straw without picking the drink up.

He bit the top off his ketchup sachet, again one handed, and worked his finger and thumb along to squeeze out the condiment. Everything took a little longer than before. When he swallowed he sipped often from his drink to help things down a little.

It was a shock to see the rapidity of deterioration.

'What can I do to help out buddy?' Casper was anxious to be able to support his friend. These were sure to be desperate times.

'I don't know Cas, I'm still working things out. We have a visit from the ALS association next week. They have some people who will help us with any questions we've got and apparently they give great advice. Until then we will just come to terms with the diagnosis. I have the fastest acting type you can get. Not sure if that's good or bad.'

He looked grim, his mouth a hard line.

'Well buddy, you know I'm there for you. Whatever you go for, I'm gonna be around to help.'

'Thanks dude, I'll look forward to making you pay for that; I promise.'

Seeing Laodicea

They spoke at length about what they both knew already. It was a grim subject, and included things like Sawyer, life insurance, work handovers, nursing and of course Chip's legacy arrangements. Casper agreed to oversee disposal of his assets exactly as he desired and they set a time to discuss the detail. It was becoming alarmingly clear to both of them that time was short.

As they left the building Casper felt a little awkward. Chip was struggling to walk properly. One of his lower legs was not functioning properly. He didn't know whether to offer an arm, pretend all was well and he hadn't noticed, or express empathy. He chose the latter.

'Hey buddy; that leg isn't going so well is it? Must be real frustrating to see it not responding like that! The moment you want some help just let me know. Don't assume I have any expectations of when you do or don't need help. You don't even need to say anything, just give me an indication that you want a bit more support and I am in.'

When Casper dropped him off, just before they parted Chip reminded Casper that his attendance at Chip and Faye's church was mandatory on Sunday. It was Sawyer's dedication. Faye and Chip had settled into a vigorous little church plant over at Carmel Valley where they had been lucky enough to secure a beautiful apartment. The parent church of the plant was overseen by Faye's dad, and he had high hopes for the couple's ministry future. This was especially true now that Chip's leadership and personable skills were starting to mature under Faye's influence.

Consequently, the next Sunday, resplendent in smart casual dress, Tommy Bahama shirt, Ralph Lauren Chinos, Casper slid the Porsche into a suitable parking slot in the lot and strode into the foyer of Mission Hills Christian Community Fellowship. He was an impressive sight, lean and handsome with a winning smile and a prosperous commanding air.

The welcoming team looked especially pleased to see him, showing him to a decent seat behind a scowling toddler struggling with his mom's arm lock. Casper smiled widely and gave a little wave. The scowl was replaced by a look of surprise and a quick withdrawal to his mom's armpit. From there a curious if slightly nervous eye regarded Casper suspiciously. The child soon lost interest and resumed his struggle.

The service was unremarkable except that it was much less structured than things at Ablaze. There was a lot of spontaneous stuff. People seemed to feel free to come down to the mic and say something about what was going on in their lives. There was an encouragement here, a testimony of God's goodness — largely materially — there. Casper found this stuff a little tiresome. First off, he preferred people to have worked on public presentations before assaulting the congregation's ears with their take on life. Second, he was still reacting to what he had learned about poverty and wasn't at all convinced that God's main priority for people's lives through the week was to give us nice stuff.

However he found himself admitting that some of the unpolished and unscripted stuff was refreshing. It wasn't his preference and wouldn't play well among his colleagues in the high-tech world of design and development but some people really seemed to carry something from God for the others. He found himself curiously spiritually alive, despite the grating style and unfamiliarity of everything. The singing was awful.

When it came to the dedication he, along with everyone else, was invited to stand as a demonstration of their commitment to Chip, Faye and Sawyer through whatever trials life threw at them. The parents had declared that they would seek to live out Christ's values in the home in such a way that in the course of time Sawyer would choose to own them himself. He stood willingly, knowingly. Being a principled man he would not make such a physical statement without following through on it. He knew it would certainly be costly.

After the ceremony there was a community lunch. Casper stayed right through and helped clear up. He got a moment with Faye.

Seeing Laodicea

She'd been a little tearful during the service, especially when the congregation stood with them.

She thanked Casper for all the support and they reflected on the service for a moment. Her father had delivered the message. He had given no indication of the incredible stress the shock news of Chip had loaded on his shoulders. He was a rock, she said, an absolutely dependable constant in a horrible storm.

'I guess this wasn't the week to make any announcements about Chip to the congregation.'

She said flatly, 'Everybody knows there's something very wrong with him, they're praying and all. We just wanted to focus on celebrating about Sawyer before we tell everyone about the ALS.'

Casper nodded appreciatively. 'That was wise.'

He left the building with a strong sense of foreboding. It was probably being invited to commit himself to the little family that had brought home to him this wasn't something "out there and unpleasant but not particularly relevant". This was going to hurt.

In the car on his way home he prayed. He'd asked for stuff before and was never really sure whether what happened next involved God or not. He certainly seemed very lucky, but were prayer and luck related? It was all a bit vague and woolly. Today however the battle lines were clearly drawn.

ALS was incurable. If there was no miracle Chip would be dead, as early as next year but certainly the year after. He wept as he prayed and drove. It seemed sensible to pull over and as he did, for the first time in a long time he experienced the presence of God as he told Heaven all about his friend.

As if God didn't know! Casper didn't really have a working theology of prayer. That didn't seem to matter. God seemed close, real and comforting — listening.

14. DO THEY KNOW?

Casper and Candice sat together through Sir Ralph's highly entertaining discourse on providing healthcare *in extremis*. He had story after story of life–saving interventions. The audience was moved to tears, and the affable Sir Ralph with his old Etonian accent was geniality personified. There was a touch of sanctified *roué* in the man. The twinkle in his eye, set in a much lived–in bearded face, suggested a lifestyle of merriment and no little indulgence in adult beverages. He was a convincing and compelling philanthropist, a mobiliser and a thoroughly "good egg", to use his own parlance.

In the Q and A that followed, Sir Ralph used terms like 'old thing' instead of 'sir' when responding and 'jolly good show' to indicate approval when someone else said something he liked. He really was quite adorable, the kind of person you invite to parties to lighten the mood.

Casper had a question, and not one that Sir Ralph was expecting.

'Did you have an employee working in Burkina Faso, by the name of Benjamin Traoré?'

Seeing Laodicea

'Certainly did my good man — stout fellow.'

By which Casper took him to mean "good egg".

'Do you know the dear chap?'

Casper admitted that they had met at another conference and that Benjamin had told him all about the desperate plight of the villagers towards the Burkina Faso and Mali border where he had served.

'Oh yes Burkina Faso, fascinating place; been there many a time. Elephants I recall, elephants, lots of need. We have a strong partnership with the Pentecostals over there. Very excitable people, churches full to bursting.'

Other questions followed, allowing Sir Ralph to highlight some of the amazing field operations that had saved lives, and the incredible impact his organisation's field clinicians had made.

'Can you absolutely confirm every part of the statement on that pop-up banner over there?'

50 pairs of eyes turned to the banner in question on which a beautiful African girl with huge trusting eyes sported an outsized plaster cast and sling on her left arm. She was smiling. The large print emblazoned on the 12-foot banner read:

> The best possible emergency medical care, provided free at the point of need to those in areas too remote to access hospitals.

'Phwmmph... I, I, er I don't know what you are suggesting young man.'

Casper had offended the lovely old duffer and risked spoiling a decent evening for everyone. Normally an excellent orator and debater he had blundered slightly in his eagerness to nail a lie, and identify its source. He needed to disarm the situation.

'I apologise if you are finding an unkind inference in the question. It was put innocently enough; please take it at face value. What you are providing is incredible, expensive and I imagine difficult to maintain. I just wanted to be sure that when we invest in you, the poor and the needy receive the benefits.'

He reached for a positive line.

'I am very interested in helping you but don't see how you can limit the numbers of people benefiting from the care. Surely some kind of cost attached would sensibly keep all but the extreme cases from swamping your clinics.'

Sir Ralph warmed visibly to this intelligent and potentially generous questioner.

'Old thing, I think you are underestimating the excellence of the field teams in clinical assessments and in generating a culture of sensible access by the people they seek to serve. Partnership with village elders and regular dialogue with local chiefs ensures a working model that benefits all and is not abused.'

Casper looked reassured.

'No more questions your honour!' People chuckled.

'Oh I'm not a JP; I'm a Knight of the realm!' More laughter greeted this sally and Sir Ralph turned away, both men quite relieved that their dialogue had gone a lot better than its initial exchanges had boded.

'So that's it then, nailed them both,' thought Casper.

There was absolutely no reason why Sir Ralph would lie about Benjamin's employment. He had worked for Light To Africa. It was clear that if he were corrupt, the conversation they'd had when they had met for lunch at the Four Seasons, would have backed him into a corner. Unable to truthfully escape that tight spot, Benjamin had lied. Casper was becoming certain.

Seeing Laodicea

'Sir Ralph hasn't got a clue what's going on. Benjamin and someone else in the country are lying to cover their tracks. It's likely that the whole country network is corrupt.' Casper's thoughts raced to irrevocable conclusions.

That absolutely settled things. He was off to Burkina Faso, board approval or not. There was one other little thing he needed to do too. His security clearance was extremely high and his friends within the military could get a clean line to the UN. From what Benjamin had said of his current employer, United Medical, there was a lot of UN investment in their operations. It might be good to have a close look at what Benjamin Traoré was doing over at United Medical Aid. A leopard apparently rarely changed his spots. Casper entered a task into his iPhone to check on United's funding base and the scale of its operation. This time he would have that run from a military source. It was probably time to cover his tracks.

The final "Do They Know It's Christmas?" session was given to Leona, Blair's wife. She had been present in South Africa but apart from speaking one evening Casper had hardly seen her. She had mostly been running some big women's team while the English group who welcomed Casper had been visited more often at the build sites by Blair.

Candice knew Leona quite well somehow, had apparently spoken with her in Mexico and there'd been some Twitter and email correspondence between them since.

Casper and Candice were excited to hear what she had to say. This outfit had disrupted both of their lives and although their experiences had been on different continents, the same values and vision had underpinned them.

The fiery little red–headed non–profit founder began by explaining what it was like to grow up in Texas in the 1960s where she'd had a profound experience of God as a little girl.

She named a facility where at the time, segregation was ending and the consequent massive over-reaction by culturally illiterate townspeople had made no sense to her.

She described experiencing an intuitive understanding of the value of human worth that had been hers from the moment she became a follower of Jesus. Even as a little girl she considered respecting others' rights had to be taught out of a person in order for them to become racist. She had made a stand, aged 11.

Casper was thinking of a Mandela quote. He'd read Long Walk to Freedom as a result of visiting Soweto:

> No one is born hating another person because of the colour of his skin, or his background, or his religion. People must learn to hate.

He reflected as he listened; Leona had managed not to learn to hate in a town where xenophobia was quite normal.

Candice was on a completely different track, aware that the speaker was teaching on a supernatural level by speaking lived-out truth. She was back in Gujarat listening to Prity describe what it was like to have to live downwind in case her untouchability was contagious. A quiet fury bubbled in her; God fury. Her thoughts flicked to her reading.

> Hate; hate, writes Steve Taylor, hate, hate. It's the only hate worth having and it comes by a different name.

What Candice was feeling was furious love. God's love; and she knew exactly what Leona was talking about.

In the final Q and A Leona was sensational. There were questions relating to Mexico that were laced with the fear of threats to employment and privilege. She went for the question behind the question every time.

'If you're suggesting that treating anyone unfairly because you're wedded to your nationalistic self-interest is OK, then you have forgotten that your eternal identity is to be part of the Kingdom of

Seeing Laodicea

God. My friend you need to understand that God hears the cries of the poor. He looks into the eyes of the little ones, sick because of the conditions they are forced to live in. And if you think that's OK because they're Mexicans, and therefore below you: you've just placed a low pay scale on your usefulness to God. You do the sums and work out if you'll think that attitude was worth it in 300 years' time!'

'You know I once had a guy come up to me after a session like this in his church. He said: "I'm glad you're building houses down in Mexico for poor Mexicans, because that's gonna help keep 'em down there!" I didn't know whether to punch him or laugh!'

Candice loved her.

After it was all over, Leona came straight over to Candice.

'Hi, you're from San Diego aren't you, over in Mission Valley? You came down to Baja a few years ago with Garry Manahan's church. Hey and your man's familiar too, where have I seen you, big fella? Recently I think!'

'Yes we're both with Ablaze, though Garry has moved on now. Casper came down to South Africa with Blair in July, I was in Mexico four and a half years ago. We had a long talk, I don't think I've been quite the same ever since.'

Candice was impressed to be recognised, Casper less so.

'What brings you here?' Leona was pleased to see them at a justice conference.

'Well I had a bit of a re-evaluation after I came home, read your book *Disrupted* and well, changed the course of my life.' Candice replied. 'I've done a Masters at Pacific, and gone on to Gujarat, India where I'm trying to find a way to help out.'

'India! Oh wow, I was there last year with Stop the Traffic. Shed a lot of tears! Did you know that 85% of all trafficked children are from housing poverty or are homeless? That's why we were there. We should talk some more.'

Casper felt out of the loop. He realised he was in the company of two women who were both utterly devoted to the poor. He however was caught between two worlds. He was unhappily complicit in injustice, something he was exercised about when he came to places like this. He wasn't however moved enough to do anything about it within his business practice. It was a reality he glimpsed from time to time. Mostly he considered it a good thing that he had all his needs met, and that he had something left over to help the likes of Blair and Leona.

In the car on the two-hour journey back to San Diego they continued what had been an exciting discussion throughout the down-times of the conference: the concept and early structure of Transparent Trade. Just as he dropped her off, Casper dropped the bomb.

'I am willing to put half my savings fund to back this thing. That's a total sum of 16 million dollars. I do expect you to make money, and not to lose my investment. The non-profit can pay me back my capital interest free when it can stand on its own feet.'

Candice was stunned.

'Cas that's incredible, why would you risk all that?'

'I need to be prepared to get poorer. Can't think of anyone I'd rather ask to help me achieve it.'

Candice thought hard for a few minutes as they sat in the car outside her mom's rented apartment. Casper felt restless but didn't want to rush her out of the door. Being invited up for coffee had too many complicated memories, it wasn't an option. He kept his eyes on the mirrors. This was not a neighbourhood in which to be sat in a nearly-new Porsche 911 991 cabriolet with the handbrake engaged. He was watchful for trouble.

'I don't think I can operate on a scale like that.'

Candice was genuinely concerned that in her desire to kick off something incredible she had over reached. When it was a dream, anything seemed possible. Now it had the means to become reality she was overcome by her own inadequacy.

'Then make me Chairman and I'll run Transparent Trade for you.'

It was agreed in principle, there and then. The detail could come together as the project developed. There was sufficient trust between them to make hard commitments quickly. It was as simple as that.

15. TEARS

As usual the board meeting at CaMPus Solutions Inc. was meticulously planned. Reports had been filed on time, all with a one–page summary and with any 'padding' relegated to appendices. Casper was an absolute stickler about people wasting his time with pointless reading.

The agenda was always circulated one week in advance with every board member reserving 16 working hours between the circulation date and the meeting to work through the updates, ask and answer questions on the reports, and offer solutions to difficulties flagged up by their fellow Directors.

The meeting itself always therefore looked forwards, and forwards was habitually a stratospheric climb.

While happy to comply with the culture Casper had created, there was one board member who stood out starkly from the others. One brown corduroy jacket caught the eye among richly blended tones of dark navy and charcoal Armani and Versace. One Bic biro behind the ear, among universally sported gold plated top pocket furniture from Mont Blonc and Sheaffer. Marcus

Seeing Laodicea

Postlethwaite ploughed his own furrow. Comfortable in his own skin, a restlessly agile thinker, constantly absorbed in acquiring skills and knowledge, Marcus would never conform to norms. That was why he was so fabulous at innovation and creation. Of the players on Casper's team sheet, Marcus would always be first pick.

It was an exceptional team; each expertly coached at Casper's expense, every one analysed effectively so that Casper could position them to do for the company what they would have happily volunteered to do themselves. He was a non–controlling, releasing leader, always seeking ways of delegating decisions. He would not make a decision for the company that could be made by someone else. He knew that to do so would ultimately weaken his team. He had been building strength and creativity at the core of CaMPuS for years. His key players loved their jobs, and most worked far too hard, not because they were in fear of being passed over but because they were being asked to do what they could not help doing well.

Today's meeting had a couple of odd inclusions under the headings "Cultural Change" and "Sabbatical." People were intrigued.

Casper explained as they came up — what he was introducing.

'I am re–evaluating why CaMPuS exists,' he began, worryingly for some.

> 'We operate to the highest quality assurance standards. We seek to cultivate an atmosphere of creative excellence, striving always to delight our customers by marrying innovative design and style with stunning performance, providing our stakeholders with the highest yields on their investments.'

He quoted from the company's 'Vision, Passion and Goals' paper. There were other statements he could have pulled from it but this one captured the essence of what they were all about.

'The question I'm asking is, in an honest appraisal of how we act in the harsh reality of trading life, does our essence statement hold up, or does it break into its component interests? Are we living for creative excellence, our customers' delight, or our shareholders' yields?

'I think if we are totally honest, we have allowed our shareholders to drive us too hard. You have all worked with me in ruthlessly thinning out the new projects order book, and for that I am grateful. However there has been a shareholder and stakeholder backlash. The investors can see the pace slackening and they are experts at calling the tune.'

He had the hushed focussed attention of all.

'What that tells us is that we are owned by the financial yields. We exist primarily to make money.'

'Of course we do. That's why we are in business,' thought most of the board. 'Tell us something new!'

'I want to ask a question that will introduce a serious challenge to that. How much money should we make before we can truthfully say "We have achieved our purpose?" At what point can we say "We have done what we set out to do?" Can we ask of ourselves corporately, what so many individuals ask of themselves? "Is there more to life?"

'Observe owners of corporate giants, such as Buffet, Gates, Ebay's Omidyar, and even rock star Gene Simmons. First they made their pile, then they sought to give it away. I want us to exist both to make money and contribute to a better world; and make that switch earlier than other successful entrepreneurs.'

Probably the fiercest, least structured debate in the history of CaMPuS leadership took place over the ensuing two hours. The board meeting was a productive disaster.

153

Seeing Laodicea

Casper was accused of breaking his own rules regarding how topics should be introduced. He had hardly briefed the team at all on his thoughts on the subject until the meeting itself.

The reactions were largely based on fear and insecurity. Casper was potentially messing with a system that met their needs. Voices were raised, passions ran high. Casper got truly angry and started lashing out at people. Even Marcus was openly critical, especially when creative excellence as a core value of the company was being called into question. He personalised the challenge, hearing it as if his core skill was being viewed as making an insufficient contribution to the company's essence.

Some key decisions were taken to intranet correspondence, a couple of projects fell off the bottom of the agenda completely; and everyone was dissatisfied with the amorphous, conclusion-less fiasco that had wasted most of their day.

Chip's health was not discussed. Droneview, although largely sold on, was linked developmentally and governmentally to the CaMPuS group through retained shareholdings and Directorial representation. A report into ALS had been commissioned by Casper's HR team, and a functional prognosis projection had been circulated.

Outside the meeting, the board agreed to recruit a high calibre young Turk to shadow Chip through what was likely to be a rapid decline in health. Chip would receive full pay irrespective of his ability to perform all his current functions, up until the moment he could not continue to attend his place of work. At that stage insurances would kick in, but until then Casper was insistent that the end of Chip's working life would be dignified by a full salary and respect for his rank.

The board's mood was such that it did not really discuss the "Sabbatical" item on the agenda. Casper announced that he was taking a sabbatical for three months to further understand the concept of increasing ethical standards for CaMPuS and wanting to put serious developmental weight behind the establishment of an ethical trading arm Transparent Trade.

Casper had begun communicating, outlining its conceptual progress so far, but this was the first time it had made a formal agenda. Everyone on the board had seen reports and most were asking why? Questions were asked about focus and core business. There were no good answers and, judging by the way this board meeting had gone, unrest was brewing. Casper loved a good scrap, so was not unduly worried by some boardroom combat from the point of view of getting his way. However he did have some concerns about the impact on the business. These were shrewd operators put in place because they knew what they were doing. Their criticism had rattled him but he had got his way. He left the meeting conscious of the real fights to come for which his emerging opponents would be far better prepared.

The following Friday afternoon, Casper booked six weeks in Africa and India nine months hence, having researched and planned a draft schedule for the trip during his insomnia–plagued nights.

He took Marcus down to Pizza Hut, sat among its low–income clientele and ate comfort food. They didn't argue, though they could easily have done so. Instead they chose to talk about Chip.

On Sunday Casper was present at Mission Hills Christian Community Fellowship again. He wanted to be there to support Chip and Faye.

It was Faye's dad who made the announcement.

'...Chip and Faye have been drawn to the book of Daniel, where the three young exiled students from Judah stood up to King Nebuchadnezzar: "We want you to know, oh King, that our God is able to deliver us, and even if he doesn't we will not be unfaithful to him".'

His voice was a little unsteady as he fought to control his reaction both to the enormity of the consequences of 'even if he doesn't' and to the courage of his daughter and son.

'This is a church where we believe in the power of prayer. It is a time to fight for the life of our brother Chip. Come on family of

God, let's get on our knees and plead for God's intervention. This is one circumstance where medical science can only help alleviate symptoms. At this time no cure is available; no real help of the kind most needed by Chip can come from there. We need a miracle, and we need to get busy asking for one.'

'He really was magnificent,' thought Casper as the tears slid down his cheeks and he made a determination to be part of whatever intercession strategy the church called, despite primarily attending another congregation.

He also checked his diary and invited Chip out to Fuddruckers in a couple of weeks. Coping with Chip and Marcus' fast-food needs was becoming prejudicial to his health. Casper booked his lean muscular frame in for three extra gym sessions, and added an extra mile to his thrice weekly jog. His life coach insisted on it.

It was a week of tears. Candice's mum soaked her scarf at the airport as her daughter disappeared again for an indefinite period in terrorist-affected regions. As always she was convinced that the worst would happen, and could not help herself in voicing that opinion to Candice frequently in the days leading up to her departure. This did nothing to divert Candice from her plans, just made the atmosphere in the little apartment rather tense.

Candice's reunion with Prity was also a watery one. The two girls had grown very close through travelling together and sharing vision and mission passion. They stayed up for half of the first night catching up on Candice's trip and dreaming of the increasingly exciting future.

In the days that followed Candice unveiled her vision such as she had developed it so far, for Transparent Trade.

The logic was extremely simple. Produce an excellent clothing range with highly polished and sophisticated marketing. Ensure that every part of the supply chain came from ecologically sustainable sources. The company would be a 'for profit' multinational. It would have an ethical wages policy which would divide the staff based among the Western markets from the Sub–Continental production team. However there could never be more than a 25:1 ratio from the highest paid worker to the lowest irrespective of location. They had originally wanted this at 7:1 but there had to be recognition that change coming to the culture around the company would be slow in talking effect. Thus if Transparent Trade paid a cotton spinner five times as much as a teacher or a medical doctor made in the same city, they would negatively skew the aspirational dynamics for promising students local to the project. This could be particularly unhelpful if it was successful and grew substantially.

The conditions of workers and the working practices in any garment production facility would be streamed by live webcam to anyone interested enough to check. The cameras would be throughout the facility, except of course the wash rooms, allowing an interested party to select a camera and conduct their own study of how many hours people were working if they chose to do so.

The accounts would also be transparent, updated monthly and published online, enabling a customer to check whether the pie chart of how their purchase price was divided across the stakeholders was accurate and current.

Casper and Chip through their football history had access to players' wives in the fashion industry, some very high profile models. Among them were some that might be very keen to get involved in an exciting ethical fashion movement.

Prity's eyes widened as she realised the scope and scale of what was being discussed.

'We want to make a statement in quality; that exposes both the market and the consumer to competition which makes them look both ethically and fashionably shabby. We will aim to see strong take–up among the wealthiest in society, keen to be seen in our product.'

Seeing Laodicea

That all production would be dependent on OBCs, Dalit and scheduled castes was non-negotiable. If the prevailing wind of Indian society sought to block the untouchables from the subcontinent's markets, Candice's presence among them and her Western contacts opened the way for them to go straight to the most lucrative markets in the world. There would be no questions asked about caste there.

16. MINORS

Joseph and Eve had travelled back to Bobo Dioulasso from the Pacific social justice conference, which had set up that rather strange but undeniably opulent dinner with Casper and Benjamin. They caught the bus on to Bobo from where they picked up their car for the last leg out to Bandaradougou. They were filled with the encouragements and pledged support of significant contacts made. A couple of attendees at the conference had pressed cash donations on Joseph totalling $2700.

Things were changing on the streets around their little church. The bitter impact of the abject poverty that surrounded it was a constant backdrop to everything they did. The little black bags of human waste littering the ground, everywhere; children playing in the filth, eating dirt, wearing ragged clothes.

Despite the grim reality of its setting, the influence of their pastoral work among the local families was having a startling effect on the circumstances of the weak and vulnerable.

Among the men, Joseph's stature was growing year on year. Men looked up to his dignified gentleness. His exemplary character and determined, active lifestyle inspired those prepared to be influenced by him to become better men. To women, Eve was like the first rains of spring. She brought life and hope to the dryness of despairing isolation within their compounds. She stimulated thriving community. Respected and honoured by her husband, she lived in the good of God's love in her own house.

Before the church began, the families had at their worst operated in the brutal, abusive and uncontested brokenness of human weakness. Now that many had responded to the inclusive grace of Jesus Christ, the formation of character in the crucible of facing family life on the edge of starvation often threw up incidents of indefensibly bad behaviour. The difference now was that the families were often willing to bring in the pastors when things went badly wrong. These episodes allowed for acknowledgement of bad behaviours and the opportunity to turn from them. Often where years of simmering resentment and walls of unresolved anger would have been the expected outcome, now there were many examples of facilitated forgiveness and restoration.

Fathers were not so easily dismissed as obstinate unreasoning thugs, who were to be obeyed or feared more than healthily respected. They were accepted as flawed males capable of dialogue, negotiation and excellent relationships.

Mothers were no longer viewed so much as pitiful victims, who were to be emulated by their daughters. Neither would their awful roles be replicated eventually by their sons' behaviour towards their own wives.

As one of Joseph's warmest friends Stanley Wilson from South London once confided in him:

'If the pastor is effective, you will notice changes. Things in people's lives that they know should be sorted out will be sorted out. He or she will hold them to it — call them up to it. They will visibly represent Father God's desire for humans to flourish and expect God's best for families and individuals.

160

'For example, if I visit a family and notice that the front gate is still broken from the last time I was there, I will want to know what dad has been doing with his time.'

Stanley and his wife Charity were in their late 40s. They had invested tremendously in Joseph and Eve financially and pastorally over the years and were trusted friends. The couple were due in to Bandaradougou a few days after Eve and Joseph returned, and their visit was eagerly anticipated.

One point of empathy between the couples from the beginning was the fact that neither had been able to bear children of their own.

The frequent visits made by Stanley and Charity rendered them deeply loved by the community. They were generous, faithful, thoughtful and committed to what Eve and Joseph were doing. Warm relationship between this lovely couple and the church in Bandaradougou produced beautiful things in all of their lives. On two occasions something truly wonderful had happened that reshaped Stanley and Charity's life together.

One winter, when the weather was kind enough for Europeans to do more than survive, Stanley and Charity had made one of their month–long visits to Bandaradougou. It wasn't their only overseas partner church relationship but it was their favourite. During their time in Bandaradougou, a young couple in the church — very poor — had received some medical help from them during the latter stages of a pregnancy.

Joseph and Eve knew how emotionally difficult it was for people who longed for children, to get involved with pregnancies. The pain could be overwhelming — especially if the person concerned was ungracious about the difficulties the wondrous gift of new life was creating for them.

Stanley and Charity had given no hint whatsoever of anything other than delight and hope in the new life that grew within the young mother. They were pleased to be able to help out and were thrilled when the baby, a boy, arrived safely; sound in wind and limb.

At the little dedication and celebration service held in church the following Sunday, something remarkable happened.

The young father asked for Stanley and Charity to come to the front with him and his wife, and through Joseph's interpretation skills, had emotionally thanked the Londoners for their life–saving financial intervention. He then took matters forward rather spectacularly.

'We have decided to call the child Stanley Wilson.'

There was a cheer from the congregation and everyone beamed happily. Stanley was visibly moved; but there was more to come. Joseph's voice wavered, rallied and lurched its way through the next translated statement.

'We know Stanley and Charity, that you have no children of your own. We also know that you love kids. In view of this we would like to give you our first born baby boy, Stanley Wilson, to be your son.'

There was a moment of uncertainty. Nobody cheered. The people were watchful, experiencing the thrill of the unexpected; the outrageous. Awe and shock of a pleasing yet unnerving kind filled the congregation. People began to feel awkward, unable to enjoy the extravagance of such a gift. It felt inappropriate as well as generous.

Stanley rose to the occasion with a response that revealed the character with which he had sacrificially given years of faithful friendship and service to the villagers of Bandaradougou. He and Charity had been responsible for raising funds in support of dozens of microfinancing initiatives. Small investments — life–changing for the recipients — had been plentiful. So many of the families in the congregation had received vital help from them; it was fitting that something extravagant be done in return. This however was surely too much.

'Charity and I are delighted to receive this beautiful new baby boy, Stanley Wilson. We are honoured that you should trust us with the precious gift of a son whom we shall treasure.'

Stanley took the tiny form in his huge hands, cradling the baby and gazing down upon him with a face creased into a wide smile. Tears trickled down his cheeks as he listened to Joseph lurch his way through the translation.

He continued steadily, delightedly:

'It will not be possible for us to carry him back to our cold country until he is much older and in need of university education. Until that time we shall need someone to care for him in this village. We wonder if the natural parents would be kind enough to take care of our son for us here in the village of his birth? We will make all necessary arrangements for his provision and schooling. In view of the fact that we will most likely only be able to visit him once per year, we would like to add a middle name. We would like to call him Stanley Samuel Wilson.'

The congregation leapt into the air with a spontaneous appreciation of their friends. This kind wonderful couple had found an appropriate way to receive their son.

Two years later, in much the same way — this time from a different young couple, they welcomed Charity Ruth Wilson into their family.

Over the years, through advocacy, networking and inspirational communication Stanley and Charity had launched a financial support ministry in the United Kingdom, committed to microfinancing through long term relationship. Their work enabled them to send more people overseas to more places than they could possibly have reached by going themselves. In 50+ countries, countless children in families who had never met them, owed their economic stability to a couple of London–based church leaders with a lifestyle habitually obedient to God.

163

Seeing Laodicea

For Stanley and Charity personally though, Bandaradougou was special. In the richness of their relational investment, they had gained life beyond the everyday mendacity of raising a couple of kids and keeping the mundane nine–to–five wheel of family economics turning. When Charity and Stanley brought influence to the life of the church in Bandaradougou, they did so having earned the right to be heard. They were family — grandparents really.

On this particular visit, Stanley's skills in setting up projects were especially valuable to Joseph. While Charity busied herself, delightedly enjoying participating in whatever was happening in the life of the Lydia Girls Project, where 270 teenage girls were receiving incredible life–enhancing education; Stanley was deep in conversation with Joseph about his beloved street boys. He and Joseph strode around the dusty streets of what had been the village of Bandaradougou but was now an ever–growing small town. They were men on a mission.

Joseph's first love was church planting. Caring for orphans was a new challenge to him. His desire for a street boys' project came out of the pastoral work in which Stanley was such an effective and encouraging mentor.

Many of Joseph's church families were obliged to take in orphans as a result of diseases such as Malaria, sleeping sickness and HIV/AIDS. Where previously starvation or slavery would be the only real options for children who lost their parents in this way, the advent of the church and its views on caring for the weak and vulnerable impacted the heads of families in particular. Orphans, who would eventually go on to scratch out an existence without a secure family home of their own, were known as "street boys."

This was an ongoing and chronic problem. It would not be solved without being properly addressed. With poverty afflicting so many families, there was absolutely no slack in the budgets to pick up the costs of educating extra children. The new local school, built in partnership with a European team through connections with Stanley and Charity, was extremely affordable and parents were expected to make only a token contribution to the cost of education. Equipment was not provided however, and children attending the school were required to obtain their own. Orphans were unable to obtain the equipment and so were excluded. The consequential numbers of uneducated street boys in his community was a headache for Joseph. He was eager to hear the views of Stanley on the matter.

In his element, dreaming of yet-to-be constructed buildings filled with equipment, Stanley explained that something he'd seen in South Africa might be possible here.

'If we can get a few flashy motor dealerships in Europe to own the vision and pass on their hand-me-down equipment we could kit out a working motor repairs work shop where young men could be apprenticed as mechanics.

'Then if we can get something happening and manage to inspire people in churches back home in Europe who are connected to the motor trade we'd have a chance of keeping that something going and making it truly amazing — like the Lydia Girls Project.'

After several days of prayerfully making calls, Stanley's determined and studiously thoughtful expression brightened.

'Joseph, Jesus is on our case. He's got their numbers and he's ringing ahead. We have a BMW dealership ringing their network to pick up useable kit. They are willing to put a project team together. One of my guys is going over to see them next month to get them going, but we have a way forward my friend.'

Joseph's eyes mirrored Stanley's enthusiasm. They were both thrilled by the impact this scheme could have upon their street boys' futures. The project had the potential to be fantastic so it might be necessary to ring-fence recruitment to street boys in order to include only those with no other educational prospects.

The women were impressed with the men's progress as the two couples met over dinner later in the week. Their food was served by the faithful Sayouba. Sayouba had previously been delivered from a serious demonic problem, which had caused him to be a chained, dribbling madman for years. His deliverance had occurred during the birth of the church here — a power encounter that left a lasting legacy of authenticity to the ministry.

Since being set free, Sayouba had served as the church caretaker, and helped around the house for Joseph and Eve. As the early years passed, this employment had been an economic and relational lifeline for him.

More recently he had been able to marry and obtain his own small plot of land. Increasingly his time was spent on his own land when he was not working around the church property.

But when guests were in town, his help was invaluable, and he was always faithful to volunteer. He would wash cars, sweep floors, serve food and clear the table. He was so much a part of Eve and Joseph's life that who he had been in the past was irrelevant. He was just the ever-present Sayouba; a blessing — particularly in times of household pressure.

As Sayouba busied himself with the excellent fare conjured up by a couple of the Lydia Project girls, Eve sat down to eat with her guests. In the company of Stanley and Charity she was completely comfortable to sit down rather than to serve. There were only a handful of visitors for whom this was true.

They discussed the new sponsorship possibilities in the USA that had arisen from the Pacific conference. This was a welcome new addition to the work of the wonderful non-profit in Denmark led by Mads and Freja, the original and dominant sponsors of the Lydia Girls Project.

It would be easy to obtain sponsorship for the boys if an imaginative and exciting project was available. The conversation around the table sparkled with enthusiasm and excitement as seasoned, fried chicken and French fries were appreciatively washed down with iced water. In keeping with local culture, this was a dry household; no wine would be served here.

Joseph was almost embarrassed by the fact that although they had made incredible planning progress towards setting up the street boys' motor mechanical workshop project in the past few days, there was another pressing concern on his mind.

He explained that Burkina Faso was cautiously rejoicing in the news that serious amounts of gold had been discovered towards the North of their city, Bobo Dioulasso. Although this area lay outside Joseph's current geographical remit he was interested in talking through the matter with Stanley.

'The problem is that there is a big gold rush happening. The mines are small and dangerous. Many children are working there and there are accidents. Whenever they are working in the mines they cannot be in school and I am concerned about what will happen to the children when the industry is properly established. They will have nothing, and qualified experts will take over the work. There is no future for them.'

Stanley and Charity had heard of the gold discoveries and were interested to know how the newly–created wealth would affect the country.

'There will be very little effect in economic prosperity for the poor people,' explained Joseph. 'The big money will be made by overseas mining companies. They will take it back to their countries, paying only low wages to our manual workers. There will also be many experienced miners that will be brought in from other countries to take most of the skilled jobs. Finally the government will not necessarily share tax revenues with the poor, especially in the villages. This is a small government country.'

Charity's quizzical look showed she needed more explanation.

'Our government runs the military, the police, the judiciary, foreign affairs, diplomacy and finance,' Joseph explained. 'Everything else is put together by NGOs. There is, in comparison with most other countries, very little direct governmental responsibility taken for raising revenue within the country and allocating funds to addressing the needs of the people.

Seeing Laodicea

'Your country has a big government that raises a lot of money from its citizens and allocates it to countless departments each responsible for different aspects of social improvement. Sometimes you don't like it though. I recall from Bible college days in England, that you call interventions from what you believe is an over-sized government "Nanny State" activity. Your problems are very different from ours.'

Joseph went on to explain the need for planting churches in the new mining communities in Northern Burkina Faso and for those churches to begin their work by addressing the immediate and serious needs of the people in those communities — especially the provision of schools.

The conversation ranged around their favourite topic. This was the advancement of social justice through the life and work of the church. That this justice flowed from the humility, love and righteousness of its leader, Jesus Christ, and was dependent on his very real delegated power through the presence of his Spirit would become self-evident. In order to explain this powerful message, so that others could participate, the Church first needed to create space for a conversation by altruistic action.

Stanley and Charity promised to accompany Joseph on a short visit to the mining areas to the North on their return journey to the airport.

As the conversation began to draw to its natural conclusion, Stanley and Charity referred as they had before to the never-ending list of urgent and burgeoning needs produced by countries such as Burkina Faso.

The broken systems of this world so desperately needed strong leadership. Leadership that was just and built on integrity. The politics of greed and economics of global capitalism continually produced misery for people in poor villages, which was rarely if ever addressed adequately by their governments.

Stanley and Charity pressed as usual for Joseph to bring through a generation of young congregants determined to enter the political arena. All four friends knew that the true test of discipleship among the next generation would not be in the poverty and struggle of disempowered campaigning. It would come in the treacherous waters of power and success. To send people of principle into politics would be pointless if once they succeeded in gaining influence, they compromised their integrity and became as corrupt as their predecessors. Stanley rammed home his passion on the subject of spiritual survival through political success. Joseph and Eve should prepare their people well.

The evening drew to a happy conclusion, full of vision and promise. These friends, speaking late into the night were energised by one another's company. There was richness to their lives, fed by a desire to alleviate the struggles of the poor, which gave them stature as men and women. They were fit and strong morally, their minds were sharp from solving problems, and their bodies fit from hard work. Their lives were lived not for their own sake but for the benefit of those in dire need. Life for them was fulfilling, exciting, charged with challenge and agony, sweetened with gratitude and wonder.

Much, much later, as the two Londoners curled up together for the night, they prayed as they always did last thing; tonight thanking God for intelligent, opportunistic and alert church leaders like Joseph and Eve.

Seeing Laodicea

17. DUMB ANIMALS

'Deaf Cat was a dumb name for a company' thought Casper as he drove out to Thousand Oaks.

His first meeting with Bella Hessenthaler was not exactly straightforward. Bella was late, wore a wardrobe that appeared to have been constructed from the local flea market and rag bag, and gave no indication that either of these things mattered. Casper felt disrespected; his standards were higher.

By the time she arrived, Casper had completed three of his usual four stages of manifesting impatience (watch checking, foot tapping, pacing) and was considering going to stage four (leaving the building). It was annoying enough that Bella's vast schedule at Deaf Cat made it impossible for her to find time to travel to him. He presumed this included all sorts of creative thought showers with other design types, and hours of random web–surfing complete with distracted Facebook browsing.

Having dragged himself over here to Thousand Oaks from an earlier meeting in L.A. he was hoping to slip down the 23 then along the Pacific Coast Highway to Malibu beach — a spectacular place to test the Porsche — before dropping in on friends for an evening and overnight in Santa Monica. Miss Hessenthaler was eating into his beachfront, cold beer and shrimp ceviche time.

'Ooh so you're Casper Scales!'

He admitted as such, trying to hide his disapproval.

'I've been dying to meet you! Candice speaks very highly of you. Apparently you're real smart, and she says you're quite cute with it.'

He raised a warily amused eyebrow. He didn't like gushing, and she was a gusher.

'Have you had lunch?'

A sore point; he had skipped lunch in order to make the meeting on time. In the 20 minutes she had spent messaging her sister or playing with design boards or whatever, he could have dropped into Panda Express for another naughty fast food assault on his system.

'I bet she's got tofu or something awful tucked away in some hell-hole of an office kitchen used by crazy artistic types that never wash anything,' he thought unkindly.

'I've got some hummus and bread sticks in the back if you're starving.' Bella smiled winningly.

Hummus! Worse than tofu in his opinion; and even more likely to be crawling with Listeria!

'Oh no, I'm just fine.' Casper's tone was sharp. 'Why don't we get right down to talking?' He shuddered inwardly at the close escape.

'OK, I held on for you so if you don't mind I'll fix myself something.'

With that she disappeared again, leaving Casper alone in the brightly coloured, zany and irritatingly unmanned reception area of Deaf Cat Design. Their logo, a cartoon marmalade cat with a red spotted kipper tie, sporting an ear trumpet, were a complete turn off. The whole situation was going from bad to worse.

The lime green curtains and orange carpet, yellow bean-bags, glass topped coffee tables and white leather easy chairs annoyed him. It was possible to clash with most of it just by wearing a tie in a grown up colour. Bella's eccentric attire began to jar even more.

The push button reception phone that he'd used to summon Bella — eventually — also annoyed him. Push 1 for Web Design Team, 2 for Graphic Design Team, 3 for Publishing, 4 for Bespoke Stationery, 5 for Video and Photography etc. Glancing down the list he was surprised there was no option for 'anything else'.

There were a few examples of Deaf Cat's work on the walls and in journals scattered around. For lack of anything else to do, he flicked through, immediately both impressed and perplexed that some household brands found Deaf Cat to be their designer of choice.

Apparently there was an army of home-office based web designers and photo and video editors with studios up in places like Arrowhead and Tahoe. They turned out A-grade fancy-shmancy graphics for all kinds of products and services.

Deaf Cat had won a shed load of industry awards for employee relations as well as their work, so it was clear that they knew what they were doing and could hire the best. Casper scratched his head as he regarded the wacky reception area and compared it to the opulent elegance of the CaMPuS foyer experience. 'It's a hot mess', he mused, 'a hot mess'.

Bella was back to irritate him again. Casper was already starting to understand that the dynamics of working with volunteers brought with it as many challenges as it did benefits. Here was a woman whose company he would be unlikely to keep in any other context, from a world which was an anathema to his.

He hadn't chosen Bella, Candice had. He wasn't paying her so he had no control. Bella wasn't motivated by money at all, and in fact had no need of it. She just wanted to help her friend Candice, as in fact did he.

As their conversation progressed it became obvious that Bella had no discernible Christian faith, swore like a trawler–man; was lewd, rude, loud and proud to be a lesbian. It was clear that she took a view that people of faith were dumb throwbacks, kinda quaint in their retro morality, irrelevant and oppressive. To her metropolitan, inclusive, tolerant new orthodoxy, Christians were heretics and — if she had her way — ought really to be publicly routed at every debating opportunity.

That she was handling Candice's explicitly faith–based communications was a remarkable piece of inconsistency; but from Bella's perspective, nothing needed to line up. Even being bound by the rigidity of personal consistency was another important characteristic of modernity against which she was in open rebellion. She refused even to be bound by her own rules.

Where her world embraced Candice's was that Candice, a fellow ex Aztec cheerleader, was trying to make a difference. The more she read and published Candice's blogs and articles, the more her care for the Hindu untouchables resonated with Bella.

Bella very much wanted to see underprivileged and oppressed victims of the Hindu caste system — which she viewed as yet another wacky organised religion — receive help. She could achieve this within her world of art exhibitions, photo shoots, demographic studies and thought showers. If she could make a difference through Candice while making minimal changes to her own life, it was a perfect fit for her philosophical position.

Things had been looking good — until today. Now she was being forced into relationship with this smug prig from an Ivy League, who'd marched in here, looked down his long handsome nose and pitched in about how he'd started to take Jesus more seriously since he'd got to know Candice. Idiot! What made people like him assume that because she was interested in helping his Christian girlfriend liberate the poor she must be a paid up Evangelical? He could not have started from a worse angle. She decided to give him a real hard time.

'Too bad Candice went back before she could get to my wedding.'

'Oh she didn't mention you were getting married!'

'Not her kind of wedding I guess.'

'How do you mean? I'm sure Candice would be up for anything — especially seeing an old friend get married.'

'I mean that I'm marrying my long–term girlfriend.'

'Uh... oh I see, ahem, yeah,' Casper was stunned. 'I guess she might just find that a little exotic! Does she know the girl?'

Casper had recovered himself sufficiently to fix the stupid dumbass look on his face as he reassessed his original assumptions about Bella. He groaned inwardly while recounting the way he'd started the conversation. He began immediately to conduct a credibility salvage operation that had to start with an assessment of how much of a relational wreck he'd achieved with Bella.

'How does your church handle same–gender relationships and weddings and all?'

'Church! Are you kidding? I wouldn't go in a church to escape a swarm of bees!'

Casper smirked. Good metaphor; maybe he could like her after all. He tried a recovery track that explained his assumptions, carefully keeping his face non–judgemental; his tone earnest and interested.

Seeing Laodicea

'So how come you're involved in Candice's mission work? I mean all that stuff you write seems to come straight out of a theological background.'

'Theology my ass! I just do the window dressing on Candice's words. I don't really mind that she's got an imaginary friend if that works for her. My friends tend to have flesh and blood, and most of them are a lot more tolerant than your Jesus. It's all bullshit to me but if it gets you helping communities then I can just about put up with it.'

This explained quite succinctly that his initial assumptions about Bella had made him look like a complete plum from the outset. It was as bad a start as he'd suspected it might be from the moment she'd come out to him.

Now that she had grabbed the new moral high-ground, Casper found himself neatly pigeon holed. He was firmly installed in Bella's "has an imaginary and obnoxiously intolerant friend" category alongside Candice. Except that Candice clearly had some redeeming features. If he had any from Bella's perspective, they still remained to be seen.

'Congratulations anyway I guess,' said Casper, trying one of his forced, yet still charming smiles. 'Since I'm clearly a witch-burning inquisitor, be careful you don't rile me or I'll fetch my ducking stool out of the car and get started on you and your fiancée. There's a lot to be said for us unreconstructed medieval Europeans, we reserve the right to oppress.'

Casper's genial, good looking black face looked about as European as Obama's. Bella's stance softened instantly. He wasn't the buttock-clenching lightweight she'd taken him for, maybe she'd made some assumptions too.

'Let's see if we can focus on something we don't need to go to war over. How do we get some justice into global capitalism?'

The tension was broken and with both parties somewhat more mutually respectful, they got to work on plans for deconstructing the US fashion industry with a wrecking ball to be known as Transparent Trade.

Bella, now within her specialism began to demonstrate to Casper that you didn't have to dress smart to be smart. Having established — thankfully without the use of design boards — the core message of their brand, she suggested the two look for a cultural precedent that had changed societal behaviour through a successful advertising campaign. Curiously, despite the wealth of anti-poverty campaign material available, they fastened on Lynx, a historical campaign group that was committed to the abolition of the fur trade.

Lynx, a breakaway organisation from Greenpeace, formed in 1985. It fought for cultural change in the UK with a brutality that swept its opponents away.

Bella looked at the incredible progress of the campaign, along with its weaknesses, strengths, effectiveness and the longevity of its influence.

The charity had seen amazing success in the 1990s at which point its shock tactics converted fur wearers from classy sophisticates to social pariahs pretty much overnight. At that stage it seemed like everybody wanted to be a part of the social reform. Leading politician Neil Kinnock, pop star Elton John, and a host of other celebrities had joined the ranks of Lynx supporters.

Celebrity photographer David Bailey took a shot, styled by pro bono work from Yellowhammer, an ad agency, that was posted all over Britain. A model in a tight dress and killer heels with a beautiful pair of legs was pictured dragging a fur coat along a catwalk, leaving a trail of blood. The caption on the posters read: It takes up to 40 dumb animals to make a fur coat, but only one to wear it.

As they surfed and clicked their way through the historic material the two Transparent Trade plotters looked thoughtful, impressed. Another poster depicted a woman in a fur coat, captioned, "Rich

Bitch"; and a photograph of a dead, bloody fox, captioned, "Poor Bitch".

Casper whistled gently as he considered the boldness of the campaigners and the impact of these statements.

When five of the world's most prominent supermodels had alluringly posed with a placard; I'd rather go naked than wear fur in 1994, it was the pinnacle of the anti–fur campaign. Naomi Campbell, Elle Macpherson, Christy Turlington, Claudia Schiffer and Cindy Crawford were each iconic celebrities, and their influence had others rushing to join the anti–fur protests. Wearing fur became almost a social crime and those thought to be guilty risked the abuse of strangers on the street. The fur trade became "The Bloody Fur Trade" — something that most would say should be stopped.

They browsed on, looking for weaknesses. These became apparent almost immediately. Making powerful committed enemies and cosying up to the fickle mercenaries of fashion for the war had collapsed first some of the credibility and then the finances of the charity.

The financial hammer blow fell for Lynx in 1992 when the UK charity had lost a libel suit brought by a mink factory. They could expect no mercy over the £500,000 damages and costs payable, and even the appeals of celebrities could not save them. Lynx had virtually single–handedly brought the fur industry in Britain to its knees and mercilessly watched leading companies go to the wall as a result of the ferocity of its media campaign. Its enemies had learned well how to fight.

Without the drive, energy and imagination of Lynx and its backers, anti–fur activists rapidly lost the ground they had gained.

Along the way, an important wreck was credibility. Of the five super models that posed for the Lynx anti–fur campaign, four went on to model fur. Only Christy Turlington remained faithful to the abolition of fur.

Time and lack of continued momentum ate away at the freshness of the message. A generation grew up un-influenced by the shock tactics of Lynx's early years. The vociferous poster messages of Lynx's initial successors lost the shock chic combination and gained all the eye candy styling appeal of a vivisection lab.

As fur trade opponents began to take up the stance of some kind of abattoir fatwa, people lost interest. As she expertly reviewed their advertising materials, Bella imagined the audience recoiling from the images rather than embracing the message. Thus the brilliant work of Yellowhammer and Bailey did not carry on into the new century.

As he listened to the effortless yet tenacious grip Bella held on the ethereal science of mass communication, he began to realise he had been far too quick to dismiss her. To blunder inexpertly into the task of re-engineering a fiercely contested multi-million dollar commercial battleground would be business suicide.

She decided that what they needed was an appealing yet punchy blend of shock and allure. If it wasn't sexy it wouldn't sell. If it wasn't shocking it wouldn't impact. She made suggestions around beautiful garments carrying what at first looked like the brand hallmarks of opponents, but on closer inspection, would be made up of the tales of suffering arising from the margins those companies enjoyed.

She chose the simple legend SCHMUCK as the demolition ball. Targeted industrial espionage combined with existing footage of suppliers' treatment of workers would be made available online linked specifically to the ads. Brands would be challenged to expose their figures in response to the transparency of Candice's Living Dälights. The plan would be to jealously guard their transparency values and invite others to clean up their act.

The campaign outcome would begin with those who handed over their cash to unscrupulous global villains who caused suffering, starvation and early death to beautiful people elsewhere in the global village. To be conned into doing this would make the customer a "Schmuck".

Seeing Laodicea

Iconic celebrities complicit in the exploitation would become "Schmuck Spreaders", and the companies themselves "Schmuck Rakers". They had an aggressive campaign essence.

Pleased with their philosophical and draft planning progress, Bella offered Casper a joint. He declined, and quickly left the building; quite glad to get out of there.

Casper drove down the windy and spectacular 23, observing the deep blue waters appearing and disappearing as he rounded hairpin bends topped by craggy outcrops, green hills and palm trees.

Somehow this meeting had spectacularly lifted his spirits. Truly it had been a mismatch of opposites. However, he was very much inspired by this crazy bohemian design guru, however much she drove him nuts.

His core 'make it happen' skills were stimulated towards dynamic action, and he was certain that Bella was grappling with similar feelings of confusion. She didn't like him but could not deny that he was a good man to have on the team, and her body language had changed dramatically while they were together.

Casper was pretty certain that he had the budget and the contacts for Transparent Trade to quickly become a serious player. He would also need to form partnerships, probably covertly, with organisations like Human Rights Watch.

His history of scaling and grasp of global production would equip him for effective collaboration with the industrious Indian work force Transparent Trade was first planning to benefit. This gave him confidence that he could hit delivery targets even if demand spiked massively and early. He had learned that people will pay what it costs to get what they want. If demand exceeds supply, the product becomes exclusive and even more desirable.

Casper, sat at a delightful beach front Mexican diner and mentally drew up a list of key roles that would need to come together in the USA.

It was a wonderful place to sit and think, the fare sensational and Casper found himself lost in reverent appreciation. The Ceviche burst wonderfully onto his grateful palate. Lime sweetened with orange, mixed with Clamato and spiked with chilli dressed the tender shrimp to gentle yet piquant perfection. The crunch of tostado combining with the rich softness of avocado and of perfectly ripened tomato gave textured diversity and freshness. The condensation trickled down the outside of his ice cold glass of Sculpin IPA. He lifted it and luxuriated in the sensation of its quenching effect. Life at this moment was good.

As he scribbled furiously on his Galaxy Note both his intellect and his taste buds were in heaven. A young man, fully alive — doing something transformative, risky and exciting. This felt like a true act of worship, a communion of transcendence in an atmosphere of beauty. This was what he was born for. It was an experience of God's good, perfect and pleasing will for him. And it involved a girl who liked girls. Odd.

Seeing Laodicea

18. DEATH BY FAITH

At the weekend Casper looked in on Chip and Faye's church. He was due to meet up with his own pastor Rick to process how he was doing emotionally regarding Chip. He also felt the need to run his thoughts regarding aggressive campaigning with Transparent Trade, homosexual ministry partners and corruption in Christian humanitarian NGOs past his spiritual overseer. Rick was more than happy for Casper to go along to Mission Hills Christian Community Fellowship in support of his friend — or in fact for any other reason.

Chip and Faye's church called a time of fasting and prayer to focus on Chip's urgent and extreme need for healing. As before, among this earnest and expressively worshipful family of believers, Casper was moved to tears. These people really cared. He felt as at home as when he attended Ablaze.

At the end of the service Casper caught up to the now very unsteady Chip, manfully though shakily maintaining his feet on his determined progression towards the exit. A woman in her early 60s with a particularly fixed and eagerly assertive face was animatedly speaking to his friend. Faye stood patiently close by.

Seeing Laodicea

Her body language, completely ignored by the woman speaking with Chip, conveyed brusque urgency.

'By his stripes we are healed, this is the time when you need to stand on his promise. Have faith, don't waver, don't take your eyes off him or you'll sink. Claim that promise and he will turn it around for you.

'It is not God's will that anyone should be sick. I'm gonna get the church elders to anoint you with oil and Jesus will make you well again. You gotta have enough faith Chip you just gotta believe it!'

She was pretty sure of her stuff — impressively full of certainty.

'The leaders have already anointed me with oil and they have prayed that I will be well again, exactly as the bible says they should.'

Chip spoke gently, with a touch of disappointment, as if his lack of healing was a bit of a let–down for her.

She wasn't finished yet.

'You need to hold on to that promise. With his stripes we are healed. You need to have the faith to claim your healing. He doesn't want this infirmity for you!'

Faye moved between the two, smiling but her manner was flat and final.

'We really have to go, thanks for your advice. Please keep praying for us.'

Casper had caught enough to pick up the way in which this well–meaning theological airhead had placed responsibility for Chip's healing squarely on his ability to work up enough faith. She had neatly added to his stress by suggesting that not only was his body failing him but he was also falling short of the faith challenge required to claim his rights in the cross of Christ.

Casper found it necessary to get involved.

'Lady, pardon me if... well I don't mean to be rude but you need to be careful what you're saying. That was extremely unhelpful for Chip and Faye back there. He doesn't need that kind of talk.'

'Well young man, I don't think you understand.' She smiled sweetly, patronisingly. 'I never get sick, and the reason why is that I'm cleansed by the Word. If ever I start to feel unwell I just take it to the Lord. It is a matter of having enough faith.'

Casper could see that it was more a matter of having enough ignorance.

'Lady, you're... what are you? You must be over 60 years old.' He gave a low whistle, blew out his cheeks and feigned concern.

'Pretty soon now you're gonna wind up dead of something — unless you're the only exception since the ascension. Every single person Jesus healed went on to die of something else. Maybe there are some holes in your theory of what God wants for you and what Jesus' stripes achieved.'

The woman looked at him pityingly and refrained from further comment.

Casper caught up once again with Chip and Faye. He invited Chip out for a lunchtime burger and catch–up in the week. There was a slight check in the reaction of both. Chip explained.

'I'm having difficulty eating now so you may need to be prepared to help out.'

'Oh sure it wouldn't be that big of a deal for me, glad you feel able to ask.'

Actually it was quite a big deal for Casper and he had to work hard to hide his shock. This was his friend and the thought of him having to be fed was a big adjustment. Casper tried to grasp how it must feel to experience your extremities, then your limbs losing their ability to respond to your brain. He concluded that it must be terrifying and alert to the new dynamics of life dominating Chip's world, put some extra effort into understanding how the rest of this conversation might go.

Chip smiled as he made the announcement. The walk to the car was slow, and occasionally Chip had needed an arm.

Then the next a shock.

'Faye is pregnant.'

'Congratulations, wow — like your work! Way to go Chip!'

There was no other possible response and Casper went with the joy of new life in tough circumstances.

'Is this a planned thing?' He smiled delightedly to soften the question.

'Yes we talked about it, and decided that we wanted another child. Although it will give us some additional challenges, we very much want a sibling for Sawyer.'

Casper was genuinely impressed and delighted. The natural drift of their conversation took them to due dates (five months hence), child care, gender (girl) and ongoing support.

Chip explained that the ALS Association had been amazing. They knew about and were prepared to provide some of the smaller things that could make a huge difference. Special card holders to facilitate Chip's continued enjoyment of board games. They also installed a clever toilet which combined the properties of a bidet with the flush, allowing Chip to be keep clean without always having someone wipe round after him.

Having assessed the suitability of their current property, ALSA had recommended that they get somewhere bigger — the need for wheelchair access was becoming increasingly imminent. Chip and Faye began to make inquiries. A friend who had a larger house was prepared to put it on the market to make it easy for them to purchase it. Faye and Chip had been to look around.

They agreed that the house had more room, but it was on three floors and while an elevator could be fitted, Faye thought it might be awkward.

It also felt like they were making it happen 'in their own strength.' It was a bit too pragmatic. They had received some assurance in prayer that God would provide the exact place where they should live. This didn't actually feel like God's provision ought to feel.

Maybe if they left room for God to make a move then they would experience some blessing. Faye had been reading about Abraham and his attempt to fulfil God's promise to him of a son, by sleeping with his wife's servant and producing Ishmael. It had been some time later that God honoured his promise by miraculously giving them Isaac naturally through Sarah's ageing body. Abraham and Sarah's more pragmatic solutions were faithless and had done incredible damage to God's best for them.

Chip and Faye continued to look for places and found one that was perfect but far too expensive. Very quickly after establishing these facts, a friend had contacted the couple with a desire to make a large personal donation specifically to help out if there was a need for a property upgrade. Against a backdrop of storm clouds, the sharp brightness of God's presence in blessing lit up their lives.

More amazing news came through. The Big Green Football Team had held a testimonial in honour of Chip. The proceeds paid for the installation of a lift in the new house. Chip and Faye's savings took care of the wet room adaptations. Some of the young people from Mission Hills, including Faye's niece, put in a huge effort to raise $5000 for an electric mobility chair designed specifically for ALS sufferers. This would give him the best possible independence when he lost the ability to walk.

A specially adapted car with ramp access for the chair was provided by a government scheme.

Seeing Laodicea

A group of friends from a book group for 18–30s that Chip and Faye ran as part of their church volunteering, began to meet on Friday nights — to play board–games — something Chip had always loved.

The book group were already discussing plans for a roster to support Faye in caring for Chip when the baby arrived. In the meantime, her sister Joy was taking a big share of the load of caring for Sawyer in an attempt to release a rapidly tiring Faye's energy towards addressing Chip's needs.

It seemed to both men, as they assessed how quickly and providentially things had progressed, that although prayers for healing were not being answered at present, the prayers and love of the church were taking amazing effect.

Chip was incredibly upbeat about the way he felt in the face of so many helpful friends, new and old. He explained that he and Faye had been rather taken with a British worship leader, Matt Redman whose song *10,000 Reasons* spoke of finding unending ways to bless the Lord, and helped immeasurably in lifting their spirits.

'It's the line, "...whatever may pass and whatever lies before me, let me be singing when the evening comes," that grabs me,' Chip told his friend. 'I want that to describe my approach to the challenges of ALS.'

Casper had to look away. This positive attitude rocked him to the core. Casper could normally handle romance and sadness, but courage got him every time. He dabbed away a tear, trying not to let Chip witness his emotion.

With studied concentration Casper took care to wash his hands on the wipes provided by Fuddruckers, his favourite burger chain, fetched and carried everything, taking care to ensure Chip's drink had a straw. He alternated holding up Chip's (Elk) burger with his own (Swiss Melt). He found the process of feeding another man required more thought and concentration than expected. First, everything had to be as Chip wanted it, and he hadn't paid much attention over the years to how Chip made his choices. Then it was all too easy to forget to check what Chip would like in his mouth next. This required repeated questions, mainly by hand signal and gesture to avoid breaking the conversation. Finally he had to attend to his own food, often finding that he neglected either himself or Chip depending where his focus lay. He was a man after all, and multi-tasking did not come naturally.

As they ate together the conversation seemed to tire Chip, and Casper found a curious self-cancelling communications dynamic going on. Chip slurred his words more as he tired, but Casper's ability to understand sharpened with practice.

Casper's primary reason for catching up with Chip today was to express his personal support to his friend. He wanted to clarify that he was prepared to stick by Chip throughout his expected health decline — if the spiritual route proved as ineffectual as the medical in bringing healing. Casper and Chip explored the conversations which had already taken place between Chip and Faye, regarding the by no means certain, but highly probable and dreadful prognosis.

Casper committed to ensure that Chip's involvement with CaMPuS and influence over Droneview Inc. would continue to function with the help of an understudy, until Chip considered it was time to stop working. It became clear during this conversation that it was highly important for Chip to carry on working for as long as possible, as his sharpness of mind and passion for the job would help to keep him going. Chip so loved his work and the company he had done so much to build from scratch.

Before leaving, Casper fixed another one-to-one appointment in four weeks' time, and committed himself to the morning and evening care rotas on the weekends he was in town. Casper was prepared to put his life on hold as an expression of solidarity to his friends. He'd stood in church to make this commitment and — member of the congregation or not — he would honour it.

Seeing Laodicea

It was with a heavy heart that Casper returned to his office that afternoon. He now had some degree of understanding about the present levels of frustration that afflicted Chip and his deteriorating body. He was able to feel everything, yet was unable to move many things, with the latter condition inexorably increasing. His mind was as sharp and alert as ever, but his body was becoming a living tomb. Terror crouched at his elbow, seeking to seize him. Depression lurked by his side, looking for an entrance.

One more amazing statement brought a lump to Casper's throat and on recollection brought tears to his eyes.

'If I am to die of this, at least I can see it coming; there is a positive in that. I am determined to die well, and full of faith.'

A half–night prayer meeting had been called, specifically for the close, sporting and board game–playing friends around Chip and Faye. Casper committed to join in.

19. SHAKES

Benjamin Traoré had landed a big score. He hurried through the maddening procedures at Lagos, switching from his chartered flight to the scheduled airline.

He was excited to be taken seriously by a senior Islamic cleric; this was a new and potentially stratospheric switch up. If ever there were a time for him to raise his game, this was it.

Benjamin's cultured appearance broke into a cheeky smile as he considered the name of his host. The unfortunate combination of Sheikh Myassa's name and title had all the hilarious phonetic misfortune of a Monty Python Roman dignitary. He had Googled the fellow just in case it was a crude joke. Having done so, and seen how the credentials added up, he was aware, somewhat giddily, that he was meeting with one of the richest men on earth.

The first contact had come through a senior colleague on the Sahel Action team at the UN. This colleague indicated that an approach had been made towards funding significant increases in the availability of anti-retroviral medication for the Middle East and Africa. United Medical was the natural first choice non-profit to handle it. Benjamin's considerable expertise and experience in grappling with the supply of these expensive and vital medicines made him an outstanding candidate for the consultation.

After what seemed very little time from initial email conversations, first class Qatar Airways tickets were forwarded to him and Benjamin was invited to Doha's West Bay for an initial exploratory meeting.

He imagined that the villa to which he was invited would be the very epitome of opulence, given the wealth of the host. It would be staffed by Europeans and Asians whom he should treat with deferential respect. Qatari men would be instantly recognisable because they wore white robes with a black iqal — the thick band which held their head cloth in place. Benjamin had been advised that Qatari men should be treated as deities.

The Dubai–like West Bay area of Doha where he knew he would be heading, was apparently something to behold. He was looking forward to seeing it, having been sufficiently impressed by the results Google Images had to offer.

On arrival at the brand–new Hamad International airport, he was pleased to see a ten–inch tablet held up bearing the legend 'Benjamin Traoré — United Medical' typed in a large font (good idea he thought). He headed eagerly with the bearer through the exit doors to a Black Lane limousine.

His greeter, Jurgen Feihl, a German ex–pat responsible for European and American corporate relations, explained that he had been assigned to look after Benjamin and was very keen to show him around before the meeting. Apparently the Sheikh had flown back from Milan only the previous day and would not be available until after the noon siesta.

The two men climbed into the back of the limo which immediately sped away as its liveried driver expertly negotiated a traffic system which appeared to have no speed limits.

Unusually the vehicle was a VW Phaeton, one that Benjamin had never experienced before. It appeared to be very similar to a Bentley, and went like a scalded cat.

Having settled into the leather-faced luxury of his ride, Benjamin was treated to a potted history of Doha by a superbly eloquent Jurgen.

'They have replaced the old airport despite the fact that it had plenty of land available for extension and had already been expanded numerous times. The Qatari way is "tear down and make new".'

As they progressed along a new smooth highway, Jurgen pointed out the many malls and developments springing up — each impressive and bold in the harsh, bleaching sun.

'The main highway into the city past the Souk is being widened and they have evicted everyone in its path. They are ripping out huge areas of the city, which are less than 30 years old, and putting up brand new state-of-the-art architecture.'

Benjamin regarded the landscape. A gleaming forest of futuristic skyscrapers on the horizon set a dramatic backdrop to the scorching dusty-dry symmetry of expansive villas, mock battlements and designer shops. Tower cranes, the quickest indicator of a rising economy, littered the skyline. It seemed to him that half the city was under construction. 'If they were replacing 30 year old structures as obsolete, they must have money to burn,' he mused.

Jurgen explained:

'Since the discovery of natural gas deposits on a scale almost beyond belief, Qatar has become the most cash rich economy on the planet.'

Benjamin was nonchalant in appearance, burning with excitement within. This was his kind of place.

Seeing Laodicea

'The society here consists broadly of three tiers. The Qataris own everything; the Westerners run everything and the Asians and Africans do everything. They take an attitude that says: If you don't like that or you can't live with it, you don't have to be here. It's pretty much a police state. You follow the rules, avoid upsetting the Qataris, and you'll get along fine. If you do end up in dispute with a Qatari you will lose. You may not even know what you have done.'

Benjamin was pretty sure he could manage to avoid upsetting the locals, and he had no problems with people organising their society according to nationalist and extreme capitalist principles.

They drew up outside a large building styled, it seemed, on a spotted shoe box.

'Do you know what this is?' Asked Jurgen.

'Some kind of designer fashion outlet?'

'Nice try,' responded Jurgen, 'It's an art exhibition — have you heard of Damien Hurst?'

'Of course; dead sharks, diamond–encrusted skulls and cows cut in half, displayed in formaldehyde?' Benjamin wasn't entirely ignorant of the world of European contemporary art.

'Dead period; if you ask me! And you know about the dots?'

'Er... no I don't — dots?'

'Every dot decorating the outside of the building is a different colour and every dot is exactly one dot circumference apart from its neighbour.'

'Oh,' Benjamin looked at the white building covered by uniformly spaced dots, with more appreciative eyes. 'I thought they were further apart, and hadn't noticed each one was unique.'

'It's one of Damien's signature themes.'

They entered the exhibition. Benjamin was surprised that entry was free. Every exhibit depicted Hurst's fascination with death. There was something chillingly compelling about the installations, which drew the eye and challenged the soul. Benjamin loved the morbidity and darkness of the place. It spoke to something primeval within him.

Jurgen shepherded Benjamin to the Souk for lunch where inexpensive and excellent food was served by immaculate waiters in a superb array of restaurants. They chose Moroccan. When satisfied they browsed the many market stalls. Here fake goods were labelled "replica" — a term that amused and impressed Benjamin. He picked out a Breitling Superocean chronograph, which Jurgen explained was indistinguishable from the authentic version. It set him back 11 dollars after haggling.

When finally it came time to meet the Sheikh, Benjamin was stimulated by contemporary art, well fed and watered, had picked up the impression that Doha was a thriving, booming, revenue–rich new city. He was also sporting an exquisite new timepiece. He felt elated, as if he'd been invited in to some exclusive club full of wonderful benefits and treasures. Things were going well already.

Jurgen parked at West Bay and led Benjamin onto the most opulent of the yachts moored in the fantastic marina. The Lady Masoura was 67 metres long, looked like a spaceship, and boasted a helipad.

Jurgen and Benjamin were greeted respectfully by Alfredo, the vessel's Spanish *maître d*, who plied them with cocktails and canapés. The grandeur of the lounge into which they were welcomed reeked of untold wealth and oozed excessive self–indulgence. Oak panelling and sumptuous leather jostled for attention among sparkling black granite and crystal glass. Benjamin inadvertently gawped at his surroundings. Subdued but glittered lighting gave the place a shimmering luminosity akin to light refracted from costly gems.

Seeing Laodicea

Jurgen appeared at ease in the palatial environment, and Benjamin felt like he could get used to it. More cocktails followed, and choice fine wines were pressed on both men by the enthusiastic Alfredo, a knowledgeable sommelier who took pleasure in combining particular canapés with the most apposite grapes. Crisp New Zealand Sauvignon Blanc cleaned the palate superbly of smoked salmon and caviar, in readiness for dates in smoked turkey bacon accentuated by full-bodied Rioja Gran Reserva.

The two men indulged in this finest of fare as time stood still and their heads grew dizzy. The irresistibly enthusiastic Alfredo put them at ease. There was a happy relaxed nonchalance to their manner once the alcohol and richness of food and surroundings began to take effect.

Sheik Myassa made his entrance after an hour and a half of happy indulgence. The Sheik was immaculate in crisp white linen and had excellent manners, showing great concern for Benjamin's health following the long and arduous journey all the way up from the Gambia. He hadn't been to Serekunda but had heard that the pursuit of ornithology and fishing there could be exceptionally rewarding. Myassa presented as a well-informed professional man. He had certainly been briefed excellently. His cordiality was cultured, intelligent; considerate.

Having beautifully engineered the opening pleasantries, the Sheikh turned quickly but unhurriedly to the reasons for the meeting. He was perfectly in control of the conversation, exuding the air of one who was absolutely the master of his surroundings at all times. He was the very definition of regal power.

Sheikh Myassa introduced an immaculately suited Swiss fellow named Bastien as overseer of his altruistic cultural affairs. He excused himself to allow for the visitors to tease out the details of how best some small part of the Sheikh's considerable resources could be generously made available to those in most need within the Sahel belt. Here the majority of people were Moslem and the Sheikh — aware of their plight in extreme poverty — was anxious to take care of his suffering African brothers.

Benjamin expertly answered all questions asked by Bastien. Again he found the Sheikh's team highly intelligent well–informed and engaged with the issues he faced. He was able, in the course of the discussion, to introduce a carefully prepared personal pitch; noting with some satisfaction that his emailed reports and bid for grant funding were among the sheaf of documents held by Bastien. His work — in keeping with the surroundings — beautifully printed and bound by Bastien's staff team, sought a vast supply of anti–retroviral medicine to be distributed via his excellent networks to those most in need. Having observed the rather more upmarket presentation of his materials, he left the documents he himself was carrying, in his own leather case.

Bastien explained that his own role in the matter was to brief the decision–maker, who would make that decision strongly influenced by Bastien's advice. It was important that he be in possession of all available facts for the process to happen swiftly and positively. He was carefully non–committal but Benjamin was very experienced at such meetings and was quietly confident that his work was of sufficient quality to make a compelling and convincing case for support.

As an aside, and carefully, meticulously concealed, by a conservative estimate — Benjamin calculated that if the good Sheikh came through on this pitch, he Benjamin Traoré, originally from a nondescript house in a poor Malian village would be personally richer by between four and five million dollars per year. He had travelled far.

After a couple of hours, punctuated by international calls and web searches, Bastien indicated that all appeared to be in order and he could see no reason why Sheikh Myassa could not be convinced that the investment should be made.

Benjamin beamed with delight, quick to offer his gratitude on behalf of the poor and the needy. Bastien waved this away cursorily.

'Save any thanks for Sheikh Myassa, I believe he has some celebratory entertainment arranged. He is always in excellent spirits when he has found an agreeable way to share his financial good fortune.

Bastien explained that for Myassa, friendship was important and that Benjamin should make every effort to fully enter in to whatever social mayhem the Sheikh offered. He confided his own understanding of how best to cosy up to the Sheikh. He clearly liked Benjamin, had softened considerably and appeared to want to help United Medical to secure the funding they had pitched so well to obtain.

'The Qatari royals are absolutely outrageous playboys, especially young ones like Sheikh Myassa.

'When not speeding up and down the main highway in their supercars, or partying in private clubs and venues such as this, they will be sleeping off the excesses, leaving the making of all necessary arrangements and detailed conduct of commercial activities to trusted and loyal staff teams.

'If they like you and you are able to join in the fun there is no reason why you would not be regularly on one of the most exclusive guest lists in the world. Those guest lists include European Royals and major celebrities. There is no equal to the networking opportunities afforded by these *soirées*, but it is important that you remain carefully tight lipped about what you see.'

Benjamin looked the very soul of discretion. He was exactly the kind of altruistic professional that deserved the chance to bring a veneer of morality to the existence of a hedonistic playground. Bastien smiled enthusiastically, pleased to be able to welcome the newcomer to the party.

'Jurgen will show you around the boat; if you would like to take a swim, you will find shorts and robes available. I will meet with the Sheikh and see what he wants to do for you.'

Sheikh Myassa looked delighted to see Benjamin when they were reunited later in the evening. He had obviously been brought up to speed by Bastien as after initial pleasantries he quickly came to the point.

'I can confirm that I am happy to proceed on the basis of the proposals you have supplied. You can inform the Board of United Medical Aid that on receipt of appropriate bank details we will deposit the first payment of funds in the organisation's accounts within 28 days. Thereafter on the same day of each month we will continue to fund the project as described and requested. All payments will be dependent on receipt of monthly and satisfactory reporting of the progress you have made in the form of the documents you have offered to provide. If you are able to deliver the distribution numbers you have projected we will be pleased to support the project for a minimum of three years, reviewable after 24 months.'

Bastien shook hands with Benjamin on behalf of the Sheikh, who spoke again, considerably less formally.

'Now let's party!' He was smiling.

The evening that followed was surely the most incredible of Benjamin's life. It was quite a carousal, to which a considerable number of Myassa family members were invited. There were also several extremely attractive young women whose sole reason for being present appeared to be to ensure the men enjoyed themselves. They were clearly escorts — very high–class escorts.

The Sheikh — all pretence at starched professionalism disappearing as he became steadily more inebriated — proceeded to ensure that everyone took advantage of all available debauchery, including lines of cocaine deftly set up by the girls. The evening became a blur for Benjamin.

The following morning, he reflected on his good fortune over an espresso and almond croissant, all he could stomach from the hotel's wonderful breakfast buffet array.

Having been returned to the hotel by Jurgen's driver, accompanied by one of the girls from the party; he had continued an ecstatic night of entertainment and chemically-induced excitement.

He sipped the scalding syrupy strong liquid and gathered his scrambled wits. As his thoughts came together he felt the deep satisfaction of a day and a night's work well done.

He ran his mind meditatively over a deep and conspiratorial conversation with Jurgen and Bastien in a corner of the yacht's main lounge, the three men stimulated by beautiful and non-English-speaking female entertainment.

Jurgen and Bastien both confided how they had stumbled upon the gold mine which was Sheikh Myassa. The Sheikh himself had by that stage of the evening retired from the party with some exquisite company, apparently for a little private pleasure.

'It all began with some commercial construction bids made by one of the big German outfits that employed us both' explained Jurgen.

'He very much enjoyed the kind of sweeteners we put together to smooch him, he was fed up with the repressive, conservative Islamic culture of his parents. The family were nomadic tent dwellers before the gas exploration caused the economy to boom and made them dollar trillionaires. His parents never made the adjustment to spending their wealth and the two generations were completely divided over how to conduct business.

'I began working for him, arranged a few little treats, all very carefully inconspicuous, you know; girls, private celebrity gigs, coke and so on. He was very generously appreciative, moved me into luxury accommodation, put me in charge of his social arrangements. I've never looked back.' Jurgen grinned conspiratorially.

'I was brought in by Jurgen to handle Myassa's PR,' volunteered Bastien.

'Jurgen and I go all the way back to the University of Basel; we were in the same economics study group.'

'We managed to secure the most unbelievable employment conditions; we have been treated more like family than staff!' They both laughed.

'The Sheikh has so much money to throw around that he doesn't really care too much about the fine detail, especially over what he has already decided to give away!'

'You should have seen what we did with the FIFA World Cup bid!'

The two proceeded to describe their involvement in the engineered securing of votes from all over the world.

'You could never directly track the votes to the gifts, but we put a lot of time and effort into understanding what each decision maker's number one interest was, and ensuring that he (it was always he) got what he wanted. Both men laughed, recalling some of the fun crafting their part in what would surely be the highest profile international event of their lives. A sewerage system for this capital city here, a motorway there; in Europe it was easy! The Spanish vote went with the Barcelona team sponsorship by Qatar Airways.'

According to these two, Southern European politics saw corruption as an art form.

'Fascinating isn't it that the two countries with the highest amount of natural fossil fuel cash for bribery, Russia and Qatar, managed without any inappropriate behaviour to successfully bid for the World Cup!'

Jurgen's voice had been laced with slightly slurred sarcasm.

'We both did wonderfully well out of brokering the deals. Jurgen is the master of skimming off the cream from these things, all under the nose of our generous benefactor!'

Seeing Laodicea

More hilarity — both men had been crying with daring inappropriate mirth. Life was a particularly beautiful beach, and they ran the private access to it!

'We need to start thinking carefully about how we can cut you into some of this stuff. What with all the heat coming on over how the World Cup was bought, the Qatari Royals are anxious to demonstrate to the world that they and their magnanimity should be looked after. Questions need to stop being asked, and the best way to get the heat off is to buy some friends among the moralisers.

'The Qataris are hungry for a few humanitarian projects and Myassa is their leading player. It is likely that other families will want to get into the game.'

At this level of the administrative stratum that ran Doha, apparently, all you had to do was find the right kind of allies, stick together and stay smart. All things were possible. These two saw the potential to clean up the African medical Qatari sponsorship scene, and were anxious to work with Benjamin to secure all three of them fortunes in private arrangements linked to the main investment action.

Benjamin spent the evening becoming increasingly relaxed, flushed with success and stimulated by the company of intriguingly clever manipulators, aloof from yet complicit in the amoral excesses of the super–rich. He chipped in a few examples of genius schemes of his own to impress his new friends.

This morning he looked out on a bold new world; a world of luxury yachts, fabulous opportunities and beautiful people. All of this was allied to Arabic royalty, why he might even consider converting to Islam. Christianity had got him so far, and he was grateful for that, but this was major league.

Benjamin noticed as he held his coffee cup, that his hand was trembling. Whether it was the effect on his nerves of jaw dropping opportunities, the after–shocks of an unwise amount of alcohol

202

combined with cocaine, or simply sleeplessness, he couldn't be sure. He decided he needed a slower day today.

Seeing Laodicea

20. QUALITY

Prity had overseen with considerable skill, the build–up of stock to fulfil orders for Lifted Sister, which made up the majority of trade for Dälight.

It was a significant advantage to Dälight that Candice had dropped her involvement in this part of the process. She was too soft hearted.

Prity had come to recognise, with external advice from WHI contacts, that to accept sub–standard products weakened the artisans and had the potential to damage their long term prospects. Candice had found it impossible to turn away hand–made crafts, born from hours of painstaking labour. The artisan presenting defective articles would go unpaid in such a circumstance as there was no welfare arrangement available. They and their family would go hungry.

Candice could always find merit and value even in imperfect work. Prity could not — she was an absolute stickler and self-confessed perfectionist. If a group committed to have product ready by a certain date, she required it to be presented on time and in perfect order. Any failure was rejected and Prity, with paid casual assistance from part time control staff, would meticulously check for flaws.

Thanks to Prity's efficiency and precision, the consequent quality of work produced by the artisans was extremely pleasing to Candice. She was slightly embarrassed by Prity's approach — which she considered overly harsh — but she was forced to admit that the results were spectacularly positive. Rejection was a savage weapon but used only once, it thereafter became a redundant threat. Nobody took a chance on going unpaid for a month's finger–blistering and backbreaking labour, once they had felt the sting of a returned order.

Lifted Sister was seeing considerable success, and although it took product from projects all over the economically under-developed world, those from Dälight were recognised for their excellence.

Lifted Sister's online brochures profiled Dälight's many artisan teams with articles linked to the products, describing both the plight of the Dalit and scheduled castes, and the amazing changes filtering through into the lives of disadvantaged families as a result of being paid fairly. Interviews, pictures, testimonies of children's lives visibly improved built a very positive picture. In-depth profiles of how each item was made added value to the hand made products in the eyes of their customers. To get some understanding of how each piece was made transformed a finished product into a touching story.

Despite the excellent supplier conformance produced by Prity's "cruel to be kind" regime, Dälight could not afford the risk of failing to meet an order — Casper's input. Consequently Prity built up a bank of products roughly equivalent to four months of demand. There were of course campaigns and promotions that called for additional production, but it was relatively straightforward to stay at least two orders ahead of Lifted Sister's needs.

Things were becoming slightly more complicated with the commencement of their direct online sales outlet: Living Dälights.

Marketing and pricing were arranged in conversation with Lifted Sister, whose methodology was extremely successful, but vulnerable to being undercut by the online store. With careful negotiation, brand differentiation and exclusivity of products, Dälight promised to keep both of their primary routes to market separate and mutually clear of interference.

In readiness for the launch of Transparent Trade, Candice began the process of research into and development of the necessary training, to ensure all artisans were producing products to meet ethical trading requirements.

Bringing methodology change was somewhat more difficult than Candice had imagined. Meetings with the artisan teams were all very positive. Everybody agreed with everything. Ethical practice was an excellent idea. Candice was amazed by how quickly and easily the principles of sustainability were accepted.

But Prity was not so positive. She knew the body language behind the words. Candice had been told what she wanted to hear. Nothing would change, not even one small concession would be made. The discussions were pointless, just hollow words. She broke the news as gently as possible to Candice. They needed a completely different strategy.

The management of change was a subject in which Candice had received almost no training. She had no concept of the extreme emotions; fear, anger despair that would manifest in the lives of these poor stakeholders in their tiny businesses, in response to making radical operational changes. Without expert command of the language, experience of customs and culture, and with almost no on–site presence, Candice had no chance whatsoever of bringing through the changes she needed to see.

She read up on change processes, recognising that the stages of change, understanding of stakeholders and communicating ownership by influential leadership was a science in itself. She made the mistake of communicating what change should look like to her influencers, rather than quietly and determinedly looking for and developing them in herself.

In reality she was preaching the theory of change directly from books rather than gaining the experience of bringing change by putting into practice the effective elements of the reading that might apply to her circumstances.

As weeks of frustration and lack of communication passed, Candice began to understand that what was needed was not an evolution but a new start. Once there was a precedent in place, and the benefits of participation could be seen and explored before anyone made changes, there would at least be some way of explaining what a new, more sustainable landscape would look like. Then she might be able to persuade those who wanted to be included in the benefits of the new, to make the radical changes needed to the old.

Candice switched tactics, working with Prity to identify communities where embroidery and dressmaking skills already existed. Prior to Casper's promised visit next autumn she wanted to put together some team leaders and trainers whose ability to coach and develop others was already proven. They had the first tranche of Casper's money to invest, and did so by employing the skeleton of what would be a highly skilled and creative team. Many of those taken on were already excellent seamstresses, and for now were employed to produce set garments, table-wear and bags for Lifted Sister's outlets.

Prity and Candice had collaborated with Lifted Sister and identified that there was a ready market for high quality hand embroidered items. If the provenance of the artistry could be demonstrated — and Transparent Trade was set up to do just that — then the difference between items caused by tiny imperfections within overall high quality became exclusivity and was very marketable at the top end of fashion.

India has a history of overthrowing markets weighted in favour of overseas cartels. Gandhi himself mobilised the people to obtain salt direct from its source, and to wear home–spun cotton in order to subvert the markets of racketeers protected by legislation. There was enough residual respect within the Western economies for these historic protests to resonate with a new note of justice among India's current generation. Especially so if it would speak against the global capitalist landscape and the injustice of caste. In opening up a system that rewarded the diligent, irrespective of caste and eschewed vacuous celebrity, a new rebalancing might be possible.

Candice put together some pieces for Bella to beautify and present, which told the story of current caste discrimination and how Transparent Trade circumvented the unjust road blocks that stood in the path of the poor.

She felt very good about the way the pieces for Transparent Trade were coming together. Trials on product released through direct sales and Lifted Sister revealed a ready market even for non–sustainably produced items and non–organically grown cotton. Her vision was for beautiful, sustainable, organic, hand–made and therefore exclusive product to fill the entire TT catalogue. For that to happen on the scale of her vision, Candice could not start small.

She contacted Casper to voice her fears regarding inadequacy for the task. He was very reassuring and empowering, reminding her that the vision was hers, and the responsibility was his. He had excellent people overseeing the legal governance of the multinational. They had found ways through the legislative nightmare of India's incorporation requirements. The drive for development and links to an American multinational swung open normally resistant doors. Candice's Church of North India corporate contacts stepped up, and the small matter of the majority of workers being sourced from OBCs, Untouchables and Scheduled Castes was never mentioned. Assumptions were made on the part of the Indian authorities but no binding agreements on benefitting people groups were made by Transparent Trade to them.

Seeing Laodicea

Things were looking good for the Chairman and the various elements of what really had started as a simple enough plan now looked quite complex.

Casper thought it was important that Candice should be made aware of his thoughts guided by Bella regarding a campaign strategy involving industrial espionage. He also wanted legally binding contracts with models holding them to exclusivity. Each model of sufficient profile to have public impact, because of their to celebrity status before modelling for Transparent Trade.

After their conversation, Candice spent a little time reflecting on the relationship and on her life. Candice loved the audacity of Casper's rapier sharp business brain and nerveless approach to risk. He was not reckless though, remaining calculating and objective while managing potential pitfalls. He instinctively knew what he was doing, able to quickly weigh the benefits of the success of a strategic move against the cost of its failure.

Above all, Casper believed his role as Chairman and overall leader of his ventures was to call the leaders to make changes that led people into brave new worlds. He had been able to convince Candice that this was the most important role of the leader. He or she did not exist to maintain a well-run safe status quo. That was the role of a manager. Leaders would distill the essence of what their organisation existed to do, and rally people around that, giving them the collective identity and will to drive forward.

This role was hers certainly, and it may be that one day she would grow in experience and skill to operate on a scale to which Casper naturally and quickly moved. She carried compassion and a desire for justice, a sharp and opportunistic brain and enough learning and training to make significant progress. They made a good team.

As she thought about what had happened since she had re-evaluated her personal goals, she was amazed at the increase in the quality of her life. She felt that she was living a rich and satisfying existence, with one major exception: children.

For Candice, having children was impossible for the foreseeable future. From her perspective, bearing children was a subject for married women to ponder — something elective singleness completely ruled out. Her body clock was ticking, she was aware of that, and the finality of her decision was something she revisited from time to time. Unlike some women, she did not lack sufficient attractive qualities to have a relationship with a man. The opposite was true; she was so attractive that she could pretty much have anyone she wanted. In choosing to remove herself from availability, she remained a target for all kinds of hopeful suitors which could become wearing.

Not having a mate did not necessarily mean not having children. Candice desperately wanted to do something relationally costly for children that she would be able to call her own, even if she did not bear them. That way she could change the quality of life for some kids who otherwise could expect little from this world and would most likely not remain in it for long.

Her life's work was already indirectly taking care of hundreds of kids by ensuring that their parents had reliable and fair incomes. Despite the fact that the best possible care she could give children was through enabling their own parents to thrive, she did not quite meet her own needs. Her philanthropic success did not fully satisfy her maternal instincts, and even if she accomplished much more of the same, it could never do so.

For her life to be totally fulfilled, she needed more. Having seen how care worked in various orphanages, she'd gleaned valuable information about what might work for her. She would not be able to become a house–mother even in a small children's home, her preferred option for the provision of care. The regime was too harsh and limiting for her lifestyle. The house–mothers did their work on a full time basis. She would not be able to commit herself to that role. It would intrude too much on what she felt called to do elsewhere.

Candice decided to look around for the opportunity to get a long lease on an apartment in the city with sufficient room to accommodate some children. She would not be able to adapt her lifestyle sufficiently to enable an older child to join her without huge amounts of stress. Things like diet, furniture, cutlery, bathroom and sleeping arrangements, all would combine to make things awkward.

A very young child though would quickly be able to adapt to her. She began to pray and to plan for the fostering then adoption of a baby.

Her mind switched back to business. Living Dälights' US operation was at a crucial phase of launch, with voluntary workers and one part-time employee beginning to mobilise. Candice was aware that Casper's hair-raising Transparent Trade team was forming and Skype conversations with both him and Bella had revealed they were not natural allies.

Candice decided to fly back to the States for a quick visit to cover those bases in June, also the hottest and most inhospitable time to be in Gujarat, where temperatures could hit 115 degrees.

Her mom was predictably and tearfully thrilled, promising all sorts of social gatherings to mark her return. Candice had to be very firm, threatening to stay in a hotel if mom tried to over control the diary. The excitement ebbed a little; mixing business with family was always tricky.

Air tickets bought, Candice put together a succinct and coherent report on the readiness of her contacts in their progression towards Transparent Trade, for Casper and his team to review. They would soon be setting up his itinerary, which would include the installation of Managing Directors in both India and the United States.

Casper had discovered that in Mali and Burkina Faso, where he was developing other interests, there was cotton and dyed cloth production, so he was looking at the possibility of somehow replicating the commercial Indian embroidery and fashion garment ventures over there, with an emphasis on African styles and techniques.

212

But the overriding factor he was driving for was quality. Everything they did needed high standards of sustainability and justice but their products would stand or fall on the customer's experience. Upholding excellence was going to be their hallmark.

Candice had caught the vision and felt a small shiver of excitement at the prospect of working closely with Casper and Bella, two of the most intelligent and interesting people she knew. The chance to impact the way the world works lay before them. To achieve something of excellence and to be able to explain and communicate that to the masses was thrilling to her. For all of that to stem from Casper's stylish audacity and strategic ability, and Bella's understanding of marketing and PR was amazing. And for all of this to be potentially wealth–creating for the Dalit and capable of shifting culture, dizzying.

Seeing Laodicea

21. FAKE

Benjamin Traoré was in the air when it happened. He had been summoned immediately to United Medical's headquarters in Washington DC following the presentation of his exciting report on the proposals developing in Qatar.

All other appointments cancelled, Benjamin set out via London for DC with British Airways, having flown up from the Gambia with Monarch. He picked up a copy of The Times on his way to his World Traveler Plus seat, the best that United Medical would allow for long haul, despite constant pressure from him for better. His upgrade kit of cravat, jacket and wide smile had failed to secure anything more privileged on this occasion.

Shortly after take–off while awaiting dinner service, he turned to the newspaper he'd picked up. It carried an article based on a red top exposé that had been printed in its sister paper, The Sun on Sunday. Apparently a well–known sting operation which had been used many times on footballers and members of parliament had recently exposed a UN scandal. The method, known as the 'Fake Sheikh' had reeled in a human rights organisation named United Medical. The information supplied by the patsy duped had exposed a huge scam with millions of aid dollars and the double-selling of useless mosquito nets.

Benjamin read with horror a summary with embellishments and conjecture, of his conversation with 'Jurgen' and 'Bastien' now revealed to be British journalists with comedy fake accents. They had been following a lead slipped to their agency from a BBC Panorama investigator, previously involved in a similar scam in Cambodia, again involving huge amounts of UN cash.

A URL at The Sun's web site was printed so that readers could enjoy the full video of United Medical's Director of Operations for Africa enjoying the entertainment provided by the fake Sheikh on a rented luxury yacht off Doha.

The effect of reading the article upon Benjamin was a physical one. He vomited. His upgrade kit ruined, attended by flight personnel he was taken to one of the slightly larger rest rooms and cleaned up by an openly gay flight attendant. Benjamin was surprised that he was still capable of finding this embarrassing in spite of the anxiety attack, which continued to overwhelm him.

Waves of nausea washed over his senses. His breathing was ragged and he could feel his heart palpitations. Whatever combination of chemicals his nervous system was releasing, it was playing havoc with his body's vital functions.

Cleaned up he returned to his seat where he was plied with cold water, then sweet tea. Actually what he wanted most was a bottle of whisky — or enough tranquillisers to knock himself out.

His fevered mind ran over the many scenarios that faced him in the USA. The normal routine would likely follow through. He would be met by a driver and taken to his hotel to freshen up and then on to the offices of United Medical. What happened there would depend on whether or not the story had broken in the USA. He had to sit out the journey, re-reading the article, wishing he was travelling Club or Business where he would be able to use his tablet to access the internet and see the video for himself.

He was struggling to remember what he had said and to whom. The thought of his conspiratorial and debauched conversations being covertly filmed, caused anxiety to overwhelm him time and again throughout the flight. His ability to concentrate was deeply affected. His tortured mind jumped from each excruciating moment that he could recall to each regrettable confidence that he remembered. As he finally succumbed to a fitful doze one last awful thought jerked his mind back to terrified focus. What about the girl he'd brought back to his hotel? He hoped she had been part of the window dressing because if what he'd done with her was also caught on camera, his Christian ministry, his relationships and his dignity were all ash.

Sleep fled his consciousness. Like some angry, trapped predator, he started to retrace his relational steps to try and identify who might be to blame. Just one name stood out as someone capable of asking the wrong kind of questions of his previously watertight world: Casper Scales. The man was based in the United States and possibly had contacts within the US Government and UN. Benjamin's mind moved from bewildered anxiety to focused hatred. He began to lay detailed plans for his arrival in Washington DC.

That same Monday, Casper, unaware of the attention his name was receiving from an inbound passenger flying from London to Washington, was himself feeling a little anxious.

He had two meetings to attend, the first with Chip Goldstein over lunch. Casper had been pleased to pray with Chip's friends, an activity that had taken place on a prominent hill at the head of one of the canyons, looking out over the lights of the city. Those gathered prayed together and listened best they knew how, for God to speak. They heard nothing discernible though one, observing the darkness amid the shadowy nooks and crevices of the canyon, did make a comment which Casper found telling.

'I think God may be giving me some understanding that Chip is going to experience deep darkness in his spirit. We need to be ready to stand close as beacons of light in that darkness.'

Seeing Laodicea

That wasn't actually what they wanted to hear.

Casper was reminded of those words as he followed Chip's electric wheelchair into the restaurant. Chip was brilliant at driving the thing, far better than any one of the friends who now attended the house morning and evening, and also better than Faye, though all of them had given it a go, in readiness for when Chip was unable to operate it himself.

Feeding was much easier now, not because Chip was finding it easier, but because Casper was much more into the routine of feeding another man. There had been a breakthrough one breakfast time when the time came to take the vast array of pills necessary to control some of the disease's aggressive symptoms.

Chip had always found the pill taking extremely onerous, and now with his illness impacting his ability to swallow, he dreaded it. Until the morning of the yogurt trick came.

That morning, instead of standing by with the glass of water to follow up with pills positioned on Chip's tongue, Casper suggested he bury the pills one by one in spoons full of yogurt. They had disappeared without trauma or effort and both men laughed for joy at the simplicity and efficacy of the solution. No innovation in any part of his life or work to date had given Casper more pleasure than this. Not even the discovery of the effect of applying black boot polish to the ladies' lavatory seats in the female changing rooms at his school's sports facility; hilarious though that had been.

Laughter had been a big part of Chip and Faye's rapidly adjusting life. Once they had moved into their new home, they named the place 'Isaac House' after Isaac from the Bible, for two reasons.

First, Isaac was the son provided to Abraham through faith. His other son, Ishmael had been born through Abraham's determination to manipulate God's will into being without waiting to see what God would do for himself. Chip and Faye had so nearly 'created an Ishmael' by buying the wrong house. One they could afford from their own means rather than waiting for God's provision. Second, the meaning of the name Isaac was 'laughter.' They had been determined to enjoy one another through this phase of life, however long it lasted, and laughter was certainly a feature of their new place. Casper loved spending time there.

Somehow through the increasing levels of pain, as his joints lost the cushioning and easing effects work of his now wasted muscles, Chip remained dignified and stoical. He never yelped or flinched with the exaggerated wincing of a hypochondriac. Casper could see him bracing himself, like a lineman awaiting the impact of a charge, when he was aware of something that would likely cause him pain. If Chip experienced unavoidable pain, he just looked thoughtful, always conscious of the effect of his reaction on his aghast carer.

Today, as lunch was mutually enjoyed, Chip broached a subject that had clearly been troubling him.

'Do you think there is any way I could have brought this on myself and my family?'

The words were clear enough today. Speaking was becoming an increasing problem for Chip. The ability to speak clearly came and went, sometimes depending on how much sleep he had managed to get. Bad days also seemed to come along at random. Today was a good speech day.

'How do you mean? How can you possibly have done this to yourself?' Casper was puzzled by the question.

'I mean, especially as we have been praying for healing and so far the answer has been no. Maybe God is allowing all this for a negative reason, for something I've done wrong.'

Casper thought for a few moments before responding.

'There are a few examples in the Bible of people being afflicted by something as a result of obstructing God, or of his pronouncing judgment on somebody as a result of unacceptable behaviour while they are still living. These are very rare and tend to be very extreme cases and most are more the natural consequences of their treatment of others than unmistakable divine intervention.'

Chip didn't look any less troubled. Something was bothering him.

'Buddy what's up? Is there something on your conscience?'

Chip nodded miserably, betraying for a moment the torturous effect on his mind of the depression crouching at his side, the bleakness of his mental landscape, the natural hunt for blame associated with misfortune.

'I guess I need to be sure I haven't done anything that could be the reason for the disease happening to me.'

Casper instinctively knew this was a big one to crack. If Chip got into a downward spiral of self-blame or anxiety over spiritual causes, he could stumble into a wide variety of unhelpful spiritual and emotional stresses.

'Well for what it's worth I don't think you're the kind of person who runs around using his influence for leading other people into sinful or idolatrous behaviour. I don't see you slaughtering babies or indulging in satanic curses. Maybe at worst you got involved in some laddish stuff with the team, we all did.'

Chip looked grateful. In naming some reprehensible shared actions Casper had reached him.

'It seems to me that if you're a Christian and you want to be rid of sin, then it's perfectly possible to deal with it,' continued Casper. 'Our Pastor Rick is always telling me that cleaning a man up is no problem to God. The problem always lies with whether that man wants to be cleaned up.'

'There's a New Testament book written by James, Rick's always talking about. In that book somewhere it seems like if someone is aware of something he's done wrong he needs to confess it. Once he's admitted what he's done wrong, to another Christian, then the two pray together, and the confessor walks away free and clean.

'We've lived a lot of life together my friend, and if you'd like me to hear your confession I'm happy to do so. There's nothing you're gonna say that would embarrass or shock either of us. What do you say? Shall we fix up a date and sort this out?'

The meeting was arranged, the two men agreeing to get together for the purpose of Chip clearing his conscience, identifying any relationships he needed to make good — especially his relationship with God.

Both left the restaurant much more light-hearted than when they'd entered the place. Chip had a plan to resolve how he felt. Casper had a role in addressing his friend's needs.

Later in the day, Casper checked in with Rick, his pastor. There was plenty to talk about and Rick, radiating unhurried approachability, let Casper set the agenda.

'I'd like to talk about Chip and Faye first. I'm struggling with some anger and resentment towards God about them and their situation. Also there have been some very foolish things said to them that have really made me pissed.'

'Irritated.'

'Sorry.' Rick was a pastor after all, tended to call people up to better standards.

Rick smiled. 'Let's deal with some of the anger and resentment then. Why is God making you angry?'

It seemed a bit childish now he was asked to explain to the pastor why he was angry.

'Well I have fasted and prayed. I'd never fasted before in my life. It was something Chip's church called for and because of my commitment to them I kinda joined in.'

Seeing Laodicea

'That's interesting, you've never been motivated to fast before?' Rick smiled again; he was intrigued at what this was revealing about Casper's engagement with spiritual disciplines.

'Heck no,' (Casper just modified that one in time), 'why would I go in for any of the more fanatical stuff without a really compelling reason?'

Rick's smiled broadened; this was going to prove to be an even more interesting conversation than he'd first expected.

'Let's look at fanaticism first. A fanatic takes over–zealous, usually religious, behaviour to extremes. If fasting is fanaticism, then what is beheading?'

Casper looked a little quizzical.

'You have drawn a line between where you're at and where someone who practices fasting is at. By fasting — by which I assume you mean, "going without something, probably food" — everything beyond the line you've drawn line is termed fanatical?'

'I guess from my perspective, it's not normal behaviour.' Casper was watchful, carefully precise.

'The conduct of a spiritual discipline is usually used to focus the attention of a human being on their spiritual life. I think you'll find that very many different religious people of a huge variety of religious persuasions would practice fasting enthusiastically and say that it has some merit. Some indeed may be fanatics, most are simply more interested in developing their spiritual life than you; at least until now.'

'Fair cop Rick, you've got me there.'

'So why have you decided that you now want to develop your spiritual life comparatively more than ever before? This is a new discipline for you, yes?'

'Yes it is new, and you know why. I would try anything, anything within reason that is, to persuade God to heal my friend. When I was in South Africa I was present when God healed someone right before my eyes. I recall the sense of his presence at the time, and the way in which those involved prayed with such certainty, faith and clarity. When I have come to pray for Chip I just feel empty, like I don't know what I'm doing or who I'm talking to.'

Rick looked slightly concerned for the young man.

'You want to get to know him better — so you do know who you're talking to? Or is it just that you want some certainty and faith for yourself?'

Casper was sincere in his response.

'I want both of those things and I thought maybe fasting would help me get them.'

'Then quite apart from how God chooses to respond to you, the exercise of you deciding to strengthen your faith and us having a discussion about it, are both useful as they allow us to examine how you have most likely misunderstood how all this works.'

'Great' thought Casper 'I've exposed my ignorance.'

'First, let's be clear in understanding that God does not want a load of religious nonsense from you so you can get what you want. Some kind of transaction between you and God is a warped view of how relationship with him works. That kind of behaviour is more akin to pagan religions where man–made gods must be appeased or have favours bought from them.

'Transaction is not what fasting is about at all. Fasting is much more about coming to God in weakness and demonstrating that you are prioritising time with him over other desires you might have or things you might want to be doing. Time set aside for such things is always time well spent. Too bad we are slow to spend it in this way.

Seeing Laodicea

'God makes it very clear through the prophet Isaiah in the Old Testament of the Bible, that going without a few things to get what you want from him won't impress him.'

Rick flicked through his well-thumbed bible and began to read.

> 'We have fasted before you!' they say. 'Why aren't you impressed? We have been very hard on ourselves, and you don't even notice it!'

> 'I will tell you why!' I respond, 'It's because you are fasting to please yourselves. Even while you fast, you keep oppressing your workers.'

'You see God doesn't want you going without, so that you can get what you want from him, let's read on a bit. He certainly doesn't appreciate you riding rough shod over his human rights instructions while you give up biscuits and make demands of him. He is not stupid, he's much smarter than you. You will not dupe him into doing you favours by faking relationship. If you're in a real relationship with him you'll want to be interested in what he cares about.'

> 'No, this is the kind of fasting I want: Free those who are wrongly imprisoned; lighten the burden of those who work for you. Let the oppressed go free, and remove the chains that bind people. Share your food with the hungry, and give shelter to the homeless. Give clothes to those who need them, and do not hide from relatives who need your help.'

Casper was starting to see a little more clearly now what fasting acceptable to God might look like. Rick finished the job with a succinct summary of the matter.

'It seems to me that God is interested in a kind of fasting from you that gives him what he wants. He asks you to go without, so that those in need can get their needs met. Most likely they are crying out to him for help. When you start representing him in responding to those cries, why then he certainly is going to be more impressed. There are plenty of examples of people that have stood up for justice, or fed the poor, of whom the Bible speaks highly.

Let's read on a tiny bit further.

> 'Then your salvation will come like the dawn, and your wounds will quickly heal. Your godliness will lead you forward, and the glory of the Lord will protect you from behind. Then when you call, the Lord will answer. "Yes, I am here," he will quickly reply.'

'I guess what I'm saying is that God states he is very much closer and more responsive to you when you are found to be engaged in what he is asking of his people. He is looking for obedience.'

Casper was stunned.

'Whereabouts is all this stuff located? It speaks directly to my situation. I can't believe how relevant all this is to where I'm at right now!'

Rick was pleased to provide the reference he was reading from.

'Isaiah chapter 58 my friend. Learn it all; sounds like it's an important prophecy for you.'

'Man I have to tell you what we're going for with Transparent Trade. Everything we've talked about lines up with how I want to reposition CaMPuS so that what it is trying to achieve does lasting good rather than holding onto a lifeless goal of making its key stakeholders rich.'

Casper went on to explain to Rick the draft plans he had been making with Candice and Bella for ethical fashion and campaigning for social justice among textile workers. He became very passionate as he explained how he wanted to attempt a rebalancing of financial fairness. The collapse of a Bangladeshi clothing factory with horrific loss of life had triggered a series of documentaries and reports into the employment practices affecting the industry. What had emerged from covert filming was utterly shocking. The data was everywhere but very few consumers appeared to be prepared to join the dots between their spending behaviour and the plight of the extremely poor.

He also sketched out his own journey away from actively attending and acting on training seminars informing him of how most effectively to exploit the principles of under–employment.

He was extremely grateful to Candice, and then his experiences in South Africa along with all the input he'd received from those behind that project. He had been an extremely greedy man, preying on the poor, even after recognising the worst excesses of his behaviour. He had, over time and increasing exposure to people influenced by the life of Christ, come to see the parlous state of his morality. He had come to realise that he was not even a small part of the solution to global social injustice. He was very much a part of the problem.

Even this evening some more lights had come on over his motives for fasting, and how God viewed the subject. He was more than slightly embarrassed to think of himself barging into the throne room of God, demanding favours, when all the while he was busily fleecing other people in God's presence, who were there crying out for justice specifically against his behaviour. Odd really, that he'd never seen it before.

Rick thought they'd done enough mulling for the evening and suggested they get together in a few days to talk about the cost of taking down injustice. He was concerned about Casper, who rather naïvely seemed to think he was wrestling only against human structures and strategies for self–advancement.

There was a whole other dimension to the struggle ahead of him that in his naïvety and inexperience as a disciple of Christ he had so far completely overlooked. Rick was rather more experienced in the matter of the struggle for the advancement of the Kingdom of God. And he sensed trouble ahead for Casper Scales.

22. FIRED

Faye kissed Chip goodnight. It had been a long hard day and one that in any other circumstance would have seen Chip stoop and kiss her rather than the reverse.

Already uploaded onto Facebook was the delightful sight of Chip holding his beautiful new baby girl, cradled in the crook of his useless right arm, his immobile hand curled at the fingertip with straight first set of knuckles in a characteristic ALS pose. Faye's tired, happy face peered over his shoulder. She appeared wearily thrilled with their magnificent production. The look of delight on Chip's face as he regarded his peacefully sleeping baby girl spoke radiant joy to the beholder. Both parents gowned and hatted for theatre; it was a picture that provoked mixed emotions and questions. To Casper it spoke just one thing. "Support your friends." Here came the demands of a new baby to add to those of a toddler and a rapidly deteriorating dad. There was too much in this photograph for Faye to manage.

So it was that, following their good night kiss, Casper took Chip home, helped him in the bathroom, cleaned his teeth, stripped him down to his underpants and put him into bed.

Seeing Laodicea

Faye's mom and pop took Sawyer home with them, having too held the beautiful new baby. They looked very pleased at the arrival of a grand daughter and were enthusiastic about helping out with Sawyer. Faye was deeply appreciative of the selflessness of her parents and their willingness to prioritise her needs, especially at this time, but also throughout the illness whenever pressure had come on her.

Casper kipped on the sofa, his long legs unable to find a comfortable way of dangling over the end cushion. He alternated between foetal curl and decadent sprawl, waking often, stiffly. He helped himself to some clothes from Chip's largely redundant wardrobe in the morning. He was slightly surprised when the entryway buzzer announced the arrival of one of Chip's game–playing buddies. 'Of course, he's on the roster!' Chip thought to himself. In all the excitement, he had overlooked the fact that every weekday morning one of these friends arrived to assist with getting Chip ready for the day.

This morning it was the turn of Charlie, a highly personable if slightly uncouth young friend.

'I wasn't sure whether to come along this morning or not.' He looked a bit startled to see Casper and not Faye at the door.

'Not at all, glad you're here. Thanks for coming. We can work on him together, and then decide who takes him to work.'

Casper was slightly nonplussed to see the warmth of greeting Chip expressed towards the irritatingly cheerful Charlie, who quickly demonstrated why his company was so appreciated. He was funny, caring, emotionally articulate and responsive in a way that Casper simply could not match. He was just a brilliant person to be around, filling the room with sunshine and positive enthusiasm. Casper thoughtfully regarded the fellow and concluded that he had clearly spent considerable time in the presence of Jesus. In fact, quite a lot of Christ's characteristics seemed to be present in Charlie.

During the morning routine, Chip drove his chair around using the joystick controller as normal. Casper followed him as they made their way from bathroom to kitchen for breakfast. Chip was superb at this task, judging each manoeuvre to inch–perfect perfection. It was a matter of pride for him that long after most functionality in his arms had failed, he could still direct the chair. This morning however, his arm snagged a bag that was hanging from a coat hook, jerking his hand hard over on the controls. The more severe the movement, the more quickly and powerfully the motors in the chair responded. Before Casper could react, the chair smashed into the right hand wall. Casper, suddenly aware of his responsibilities in overseeing Chip's safety in transit, leaped to grab the chair in response to the shout of pain and alarm. His inexperience caused him to wrestle with the powerful motors but even his tremendous athletic frame could not contend with the chair, which was attempting to drive Chip literally up the wall. Chip's foot was trapped and taking the full force of the pressure.

Charlie saved the day, running along the hallway and flicking the switch to cut the power, instantly allowing Casper's desperate efforts to pull Chip away from the wall. Casper then had to tortuously watch Chip's pain and frustration as Charlie moved in to soothe and comfort him, quickly bringing down his level of distress. No injury had been caused beyond a nasty welt on Chip's ankle, which thankfully flexed and moved OK.

There were of course important lessons learnt through this painful and terrible incident. Casper was left stunned by his own ignorance of the complexity and importance of the task of caring for another human being, particularly when powerful machinery was involved. Mortified and embarrassed at his stupidity and slow reaction to Chip's emergency, he busied himself around the kitchen, glad that Charlie was around to pick up the pieces. Even though he was a friend, working for Chip voluntarily, he expected to be fired.

Perhaps what he received was worse. Chip took great care to forgive any incompetence and would not allow any suggestion that Casper could be expected to show more diligence or better reactions to the crisis. He was the very epitome of grace in his acceptance of Casper's poor performance at the expense of his fright and pain.

Casper's introspection was interrupted by a smart rap on the back door, followed by the sound of it opening and a coo of greeting. Faye's sister Joy was among them. Chip's face lit with a smile of genuine pleasure. He'd mentioned Joy many times to Casper and now as they met for the first time Casper was able to pass on some of the appreciation he had picked up from his friend. It was helpful to have someone else on whom to focus the conversation.

'So this is Faye's Rock! I'm told you're the one responsible for getting her through the pregnancy and keeping the family ahead of the game over the last couple of months. Faye makes it sound like you're the biggest reason she's not been involuntarily committed.'

Joy laughed dismissively.

'You're forgetting our Mom and Dad. They've been amazing. I'm just still trying to get her to tidy her bedroom really! Any excuse to come round here, organise a few shirts and play with Sawyer will do for me. Too bad Chip had to contract something serious for me to get in the game. You must be Casper — I've seen the photos. Does Chip have some stories about you!'

She was already heading for the lounge, which looked rather as though it had been vacated at pace, which of course it had yesterday afternoon when Faye headed for the hospital. Neither Casper nor Charlie noticed that it needed putting straight.

The three men took Joy's arrival as their cue to leave.

With the morning routine complete, Charlie drove Chip to work, which he seemed to want to do. With Faye resting in hospital, and Sawyer in the excellent care of his grand parents, this seemed a sensible place for him to be.

Casper reflected on how preparing for work, and carrying out the demands of his role were contributing to Chip's obvious exhaustion. In one sense it was keeping him going, in another it was shattering him.

Very soon after the arrival of baby Roseanna, Chip asked to meet formally with Casper and expectedly addressed the matter of ending his employment with CaMPuS. He had prepared his understudy, a very capable man by the name of Dominic. Casper worked exactly to Chip's timetable for departure.

On the morning of the office party thrown in honour of his departure, Chip felt incredibly unwell and stayed at home until lunch time. When he arrived, despite the pain, he planted a smile on his face so only Faye knew how he felt. A 20–minute DVD was produced condensing his incredible role in launching the company and remaining pivotal in driving it forward.

Unsurprisingly the sequence began with some hilarious footage of three incredibly young lads messing around with an obviously home–made and barely airworthy drone. Chip was sporting an enormous mullet, baggy shorts and an outrageous purple Hawaiian shirt patterned with bikini clad beauties mingled with bananas and palm leaves. The shirt got some laughs.

Rather cheekily there were some clips from those notorious early unsolicited and nocturnal reconnaissance flights peeking in various windows in the freshmen student dorms that had briefly featured on YouTube before being taken down. There was also of course a series of milestone moments relating to the stratospheric rise of the company he had so successfully helped lead. There was mention of fundraising efforts — including a skydive — on behalf of a nonprofit that ran medical relief flights across the developing world in whose work Chip had a keen interest. Finally, the sequence ended with a tear–jerking video–log of puddle–splashing happy times through the rain clouds of his rapidly developing ALS.

There were no dry eyes as the lights came back up.

Seeing Laodicea

Chip was too exhausted to drive himself out of the party in his chair. Faye, head held high, visibly proud and pleased with the show of genuine appreciation for her husband, wheeled him through an arch formed by every one of his colleagues. As she got him into the elevator, they ran down the stairs and formed another arch from the elevator doors to the main exit from the building. While Chip was strapped into the car, the entire staff team raced across the car park and lined the road. Faye's lasting image of the evening was the sight of Chip's CaMPuS family in her rear view mirror, waving until she turned out of sight. This extravagant show of support completely filled her mind, her heart, her senses with the knowledge of how much impact her incredible man had made on each of them and how very much he was loved.

As Faye drove Chip home, Casper and Marcus — both present to support his departure — regarded one another unblinkingly with deep sadness. They knew that their friend was dying. They would lose him soon.

Across the other side of the country, just before midday, having landed 20-minutes ahead of schedule, Benjamin cleared immigration. He was not expecting acts of support from anybody.

He had digested every last morsel of information in the newspaper article during the flight. It was pretty conclusive. There was simply no possibility of United Medical's HQ in Washington failing to pick up on the news.

Drifting slowly, carefully through the 'nothing to declare' lane and into the arrivals hall as nonchalantly as possible, he noted that the waiting driver holding up his name appeared to be alone. He approached the fellow with a mixture of resignation and apprehension.

Pleased to have made a quick rendezvous with his fare, the driver, behaving as if nothing was up, quickly ushered Benjamin through to the short-term parking facility, and neatly slipped his Cadillac through the busy streets to the usual hotel.

Benjamin was not a frequent enough visitor to be instantly recognised and simply signed in on arrival, and handed over his passport to be photocopied. He dismissed the driver saying he felt unwell and therefore too tired to meet with United Medical as planned. He would call them and explain. He paid the driver off before heading up to his room. Once there he opened his laptop and watched appalled as his meeting with 'Sheikh Mysassa', and then with Bastien and Jurgen played out on YouTube. There was also footage of his time back at the hotel with Gül the Turkish call girl, but happily this was restricted to conversations related to his work at United Medical. As he had feared, Gül was also an amoral reporter but she did at least have the decency to respect her own sexual privacy online, which rather protected his.

The total footage was over two hours in length and absolutely damning. Benjamin wrung his hands in despair. It was a total calamity. All the years of careful management of perceptions, meticulous controlling and abuses of power had been exposed in one moronic night. There was almost nothing in his vast career of corrupt practice that had not been exposed by his bragging tongue, fuelled by the drugs, alcohol and his desire to impress beautiful and advantageous company. Even the anti–retroviral scam had come out in the last act with Gül when she had very cleverly asked if there was any way she could supply her friends and contacts at the escort agencies, with AIDS medicines. He was completely undone, his activities had been criminal, and he was in the United States, a place which had little mercy on serious fraudsters. All of his relationships in the States were related to his humanitarian work so he could expect no help from those he had betrayed and undermined.

Again his mind returned to the subject of blame. His face contorted in fury as he recalled the moment of his exposure at lunch with Joseph and Eve Oudraogo and Casper Scales. He recalled with absolute clarity the look in Casper's eyes as he had effortlessly lied about his employment with Light to Africa. The attentive stillness and pensive look of a very sharp operator scenting blood had been visible for a few moments before Mr. Scales had recovered his composure and moved back into the suave role of host.

Seeing Laodicea

Benjamin had been worried about the man ever since. Quick witted, connected to the military and to Christian humanitarian mission; could it have been Casper's contacts who had eventually triggered a high-budget News Corp sting? The timing of that first chilling contact, probing into his past at Light to Africa, identified Casper Scales as the likely first source of investigations into his activities.

Benjamin knew there were a great many connections between government and high profile media corporations and it was not difficult to see how investigations into his corrupt business could have crossed over into a journalistic scoop. There was often no love lost between the contributing governments, particularly those expected to make huge donations such as the USA, and the UN — whose profligate spending habits were often the subject of bitter sniping.

Benjamin had presented as a juicy bug to squash, and it was only a matter of time before he was picked up by a law enforcement agency.

The telephone by his bed began a subdued warbling ring tone. He picked up immediately, tense. The caller was PA to the United CEO, an attractive woman named Alyssa with whom he'd always enjoyed easy-going banter. Today, to his anxious ear, there was a perceptible edge to her voice.

'Hi Benjamin (not a good sign, it was usually Ben). I heard you were feeling poorly after the flight. I'm just checking if there's anything we can do for you? Do you need to see a doctor?'

'It's OK Alyssa, I'm quite capable of self-medicating if necessary. I think I picked up a stomach bug in transit. I'm afraid I'm pretty wasted. 12 hours of fasting ought to clear it, I should be free of the problems by tomorrow morning.'

'Oh alright, Bill has space in his diary to meet with you in the morning. Do you think you will be OK to see him over breakfast? Maybe we should schedule something slightly later?'

'No I should be OK to eat again by then.'

'OK let's make it 7:45, I will arrange to have you picked up at 7:15. Sleep well.'

She was gone. Benjamin gathered his wits. His breathing had returned to normal but his thoughts and emotions jumped around alarmingly.

He went down to reception and made a few enquiries. The concierge remained inscrutable through their conversation. He was used to meeting the bizarre needs and preferences of his guests. He gave Benjamin directions to an establishment with a considerable reputation for discretion.

Benjamin pitched up at the smart gun shop and explained that he was nervous and needed help with a purchase. There was a documentation issue related to his citizenship that made it impossible for him to do the deal officially but there were a whole load of private individuals in contact with the shop, for whom such niceties were an irrelevance. A call was made, a small arrangement fee handed over and after a trip to the bank and a short wait, the transaction completed in a local café. Benjamin had what he wanted to carry out what needed to be done.

On return to the hotel he began to make enquiries to discover the home address of Casper Alexander Scales. As he did so, Benjamin absent-mindedly played with the Smith & Wesson 460 XVR Magnum revolver he had purchased. It was not his first gun but it was easily the smartest. Unlike other revolvers he'd used, this heavy-duty beast had no indentations on the revolving chambers; the cylinder was smooth, brutally beautiful.

'Oh is that Ablaze Church office, San Diego?' Benjamin's excellent memory for detail had served him well. The receptionist admitted as such and volunteered her name, Barbara. She was eager to make the caller as welcome as possible.

Seeing Laodicea

'Hi Barbara, I wonder if you can help me. I'm trying to send an old friend Casper Scales a thank you card. He has been very kind to my ministry and I wanted to drop him a line in appreciation.'

There was a slight delay as the relevant database was called up.

'...Point Loma Avenue, Sunset Cliffs, CA92107,' he punched the address into his tablet. 'Thank you for your help Barbara.'

Benjamin rang off, just a couple more arrangements to make and he could put the lights out. He had no intention whatsoever of making that meeting with Bill in the morning.

Casper was also busy that evening. He was due to meet with Candice the following Wednesday and before he did so needed to clear up his position with the CaMPuS board. His preparation for the meeting had been as tenacious as ever. He had circulated draft plans for collaboration with Deaf Cat. He did not mention in detail that he was about to enter a death–struggle with some household sports and fashion brands — all of whom routinely exploited the poor, and had the kind of budgets to go to war against CaMPuS like the USA could go to war against a Middle Eastern despot.

He did not expect the level of hostility which awaited him. All other Directors with the exception of Marcus were aligned against what they saw as a threatening division of loyalties between pure commerce and ethical trade. Nobody had a problem with tax deductible charitable giving. Everyone saw the ethical trading arm as a separate entity to CaMPuS. They wanted an absolute firewall between Casper's new venture and the technology development focus of the existing company. Casper had already begun to call upon the company's buildings space, HR division and stationery and IT resources for the first stages of creating the necessary infrastructure for Transparent Trade to hit the ground running.

In the coup that followed, Casper found himself disempowered by a vote of no confidence against the chairman. The stalking horse was Marketing Director Brad Horstmuller, whom Casper had planned to replace with Chip had illness not taken over. Casper suspected that the real brains behind the coup belonged to the Director of Operations but he had not yet broken cover. For now, Casper's leadership grip on the company had been loosened. In his desire to combat his own avarice, Casper had made room for someone else's greed to grab what he himself had previously held dear. Instead of rebalancing the company to share with the poor, he had allowed another greedy rich man to make a play to grab the assets.

Marcus couldn't save him. While he had the brain to understand all the nuances of the politics, he was a reflective man, not forceful except in driving creative thinking. He was no help at all in a fist–fight over the boardroom table. Casper gave way and allowed the Leadership Team to call an extraordinary shareholders' meeting to try to force Casper away from the disastrous course he wanted to take the company along. Effectively, if this meeting went badly, Casper would be fired from the company he owned. Having recently read 'Me, Myself and Bob' by Phil Vischer — founder of the Veggietales — Casper could empathise with a fellow moralist who took his eye off the need for constantly refocused commercial insight as well as visionary altruistic leadership. He was in trouble. Rattled, he called up Pastor Rick to see if there was any good reason why he shouldn't blame God for the unexpectedly bad turn of events.

Seeing Laodicea

23. TAKING OFF

Rick and Pamela welcomed Casper with open arms. He was a regular visitor such that he didn't need to order a drink, Pamela just fixed him a caramel latte from the Keurig as usual and put out some chips and fresh guacamole. Casper settled into 'his' chair. Actually it was Rick's when Casper wasn't here and there was often a bit of banter exchanged about territorial behaviour. This had become one of Casper's most trusted relationships.

'OK Casper, tell us all about it. Why is God such a spoil sport?'

Casper found himself running through the tumble of events that had seen his world begin to collapse. He began with the convictions he'd picked up in Soweto and Botleng, covered the time spent with Deaf Cat's on campaigning plans, and moved swiftly to the establishment of Transparent Trade. The latter achieved, possibly, with improper haste and unhelpful assumptions of what he could and couldn't do with the CaMPuS team.

Rick listened impassively. Some of the story had caused him and Pamela to exchange knowing glances, there had been the odd chortle from his lips along the way, and even the occasional low whistle.

When Casper dried up, Rick flicked back through the jottings he'd made on his note pad. No tablet for him. He was old school.

'Let's see now; you have allowed what God has been saying to you through his faithful servants, to penetrate deep into your soul? And you have been reading the Bible for yourself and trying to pray. You've even had a crack at fasting — though actually you were on track for a more appropriate kind of fasting long before you gave up food! We covered that last time. God is looking for people to give stuff up for his agenda, and that seems to me to be exactly what you're doing. Way to go Casper, you're growing up son!'

Casper looked surprised. He was slightly taken aback by the upbeat attitude of his friend and counsellor. He hoped he wasn't being patronised.

'I'm not sure you've heard me right Rick. I'm facing a total disaster, the loss of everything I've worked so hard to build. I have a board of Directors, each highly talented; I should know, I hand-picked them, gunning for blood on the boardroom carpet: mine!'

Rick, still looking pleased, explained his perspective.

'Son you were going to lose it all anyway. How long have you got before that strong heart of yours stops? 50 years, 60 if you're lucky, though at your pace you may not make 45. Then what have you got? You told me yourself that you've been hunted down by the writings of the Apostle James. He's on your case, and now the prophet Isaiah is after you too! They both talk about not paying wages properly and oppressing people. That's part of what you do for a living. You've swapped singing hymns and doing a bit of self-indulgent church stuff for a radical agenda of disruption. What you are looking to disrupt is the injustice of the world around you. You have become an agent of change for the coming revolution of righteousness. You're part of God's story now, and you're starting to discover that he's got enemies.'

Casper's eyes narrowed. This wasn't going the way he'd expected. He was looking for a bit of coffee and sympathy. Instead something awful seemed to be happening. He was being cheered on into a fight he appeared to be losing even before he'd properly got started.

Rick was reaching for an old, much thumbed book. Casper braced himself.

'Here we go; a piece by Amy Carmichael. My favourite poem; speaks right to your position at the moment.

> *Hast thou no scar?*
> *No hidden scar on foot, or side, or hand?*
> *I hear thee sung as mighty in the land;*
> *I hear them hail thy bright, ascendant star.*
> *Hast thou no scar?*
>
> *Hast thou no wound?*
> *Yet I was wounded by the archers; spent,*
> *Leaned Me against a tree to die; and rent*
> *By ravening beasts that compassed Me,*
> *I swooned.*
> *Hast thou no wound?*
>
> *No wound? No scar?*
> *Yet, as the Master shall the servant be,*
> *And piercèd are the feet that follow Me.*
> *But thine are whole; can he have followed far*
> *Who hast no wound or scar?'*

Casper reeled under the impact of the words. Of course Christ had lived clean and clear of any credible accusation of wrongdoing. He was an innocent man by all accounts.

Yet he clearly had enemies. Those whose positions were threatened by Christ's absolute spiritual authority found their words and actions surpassed. Any comparison exposed their lack of authenticity. Rulers whose grasp of power depended upon its abuse found the challenge of the righteous, the ruler of all, the true "friend of the people" in need of extinguishment.

Rick allowed Casper to figure things out for himself. Someone as smart as this young man felt bored and patronised by being spoon-fed. They sat in silence for a long while.

Finally it was Casper who spoke first.

'I guess I can expect more trouble not less if I attempt to bring justice. Justice threatens everyone of privilege. We are so faithfully wedded to our own self-interest that we and our systems move against anything that might downgrade our conditions.

'God has done such a number on me that I have begun to wish I didn't have so much. I've started to get rid of the wealth I have accumulated — mainly because I'm embarrassed that much of it has relied on me oppressing the poor by under paying them.

'My mistake has been failure to bring my colleagues with me. I have assumed their collective benevolence, when what brought them together to work for me was their own self-interest. I have done a u-turn, but turning my organisation is proving much more tricky.'

Rick nodded affirmation and finally contributed.

'You didn't foresee that the battle for justice is far tougher than just change management — which in itself is a hard one. The Bible says that advancing the Kingdom of God is a fight that goes beyond the visible. If you decide to follow Christ, then you will contend with his enemies. You will face wicked spiritual forces, corrupt systems, selfish and vicious men and women. Hatred hisses in your face; intimidates your every inclination to do right. If you fail to prepare for war, you will spend your time on the floor licking your wounds and feeling sorry for yourself.

'You must learn to hate hatred, even in yourself. Your weapons are those of love and wisdom. You must appeal to the goodness in every man and woman. Call people up to their best, expecting sometimes their worst. Do not fail to warn the wicked but try not to browbeat them, or the aroma of your cause will be indistinguishable from theirs.

'You will notice Christ never once reached for a sword. He set out to win hearts, not to use violence.'

Casper smiled grimly.

'I think I have just glimpsed the rest of my life. I'm a dead man aren't I?'

Rick returned the smile.

'Welcome to the family business. Everything you do from the moment you respond to God's call on your life will be conducted under the fire of your enemies. The scars you earn will be collected from wounds that hurt so bad you will imagine there is no way you can recover. But never ever give in Casper. Your wounds will be your glory when you check in at the end of your lifetime. If you're covered in them and they are earned honestly and in obedience to Christ, you will be well rewarded.

'Can you imagine your embarrassment when the war is over and the warriors are being commended for their part in the great battles for the advance of justice, and you waltz in, skin like a baby's bottom, not a hair out of place, with a pile of ill-gotten treasures? You will look one sad sucker. If however you leave it all on the battlefield, chuck in your last dime and every bone, muscle and sinew of your being, you will have proved your right to be called a brother of the Son of God.

'What's it gonna be Casper?'

'I think you know what I want to do Rick.'

'Then you can expect to face being taken down by your board and slung out. You may be lied about, swindled, intimidated, deliberately misunderstood and misquoted.

Seeing Laodicea

'I read an article in Time last year about the Archbishop of Canterbury standing up to what he identified as a clearly iniquitous website named Wonga.com. According to him, they and other payday loan companies were committed to preying on the poor and he called them on it. In a matter of days their PR machine had gone through his organisation's dirty linen and displayed it for all to see. He and his people got a bloody nose, and if you don't mind me saying so, he was a lot cleaner than you are.

'When they come for you, furious in the face of your just accusations, every last shady thing you have done will be exposed. You will be branded a hypocrite and a liar. Your assets will be stripped. Your cause will be compromised as they take down your weaker team members. You may well suffer physical harm, mental torture, anxiety and anguish. The beneficiaries of your acts of justice will likely be unappreciative, may well steal from you, undermine you or humiliate you. There will be days when you will be sure you are wasting your time.

'Are you sure you want that? Is that a life you desire?'

'You make it sound so attractive Rick!' Casper took a long breath. 'Actually, yes I believe that is what I want. In South Africa I saw problems that could be solved by decent leadership and determination. In listening to Joseph and Eve from Burkina Faso I glimpsed lives well lived. A way of following Jesus that was much more about worshipful acts of justice than pointless acts of worship. I want that.

'The accumulation of vast sums of money has been fun, but it's not worth dying over. What you're describing is the kind of challenge I was born for.'

'Born again for.' Rick looked pleased.

'Well done son, I think you have just won the battle for your future. Now you need to prepare for war. Remember; everything you do from now on will be conducted under fire. You have already been hurt because you were lazy in your preparation. You were not expecting to be a target. Wise up; you'll get little credit for wounds acquired by stupidity.'

Casper took off into the night equipped with a gritty dose of realism. Rick's words made sense of what had been a confusing series of events. Now he had an idea of what he was dealing with, he could focus his mind.

Benjamin was pretty focused too. He made an online purchase that made him smile bleakly, researched some travel options and made a couple of online banking transactions.

Finally, he removed from his briefcase a set of microscrewdrivers and laboriously took his Macbook Air apart. Disassembling the Mac was an unfamiliar, fiddly task requiring a little online research first. He flipped the laptop on its front, removing ten screws from the base. Then having carefully removed the back, he unscrewed and removed the battery, slipped off the cables and undid the retaining screws for the hard drive and RAM.

Approximately one hour later, Benjamin was down at the Georgetown waterfront, tossing the two key parts of his laptop into the Potomac. With them went all trace of his secret labyrinth of concealed and complex arrangements for fraud on an epic scale.

There was an air of flat finality to Benjamin, a manner of supreme control. He headed into a Nick's Riverside Grill for clam chowder, sailors rib–eye and bourbon chocolate pecan tart.

As he ate, he ran his mind over the significant events of his life, from the humble beginnings of an orphan and street urchin, saved from death by the generous help of an NGO. On through school then university, sponsored by Western benefactors, he had excelled at every level.

Graduating from medical school, Benjamin had completed training as a medical doctor, securing excellent employment with British NGO Light to Africa.

Seeing Laodicea

It was at this stage of his career — managed remotely and given high levels of trust — that his appetite for the pleasures available to a modestly-loaded wallet began to seduce him. A failed marriage complete with bitter and vicious aftershocks, multiple liaisons with feckless, shallow partners — each of whom was faithful to and passionate about his ever-improving financial status — had left him loveless and alone, even in the company of a lover. The unpleasant and despotic manner of his iron rule since taking a prominent role with United Medical had left him friendless and feared.

He had become someone loathed except by those whom he continued to successfully dupe into respecting him. He hated his life and he hated himself.

Now he was facing cruel exposure to all who knew him and to millions who would only know the worst. His veneer of respectability was about to be stripped away. The world would loathe him every bit as much as he despised himself.

Far from wallowing in self-pity as he quaffed his drinks and luxuriated in the excellent meal. He emerged visibly brightened — a man recklessly abandoned to make the most of life as he liked it. But he was also a man with a long record of making his enemies pay for blows struck against him.

Gina the waitress was delighted with the tip she received, having plied him with rather too much Jim Bean throughout the meal. She had thrown in an Irish coffee on the house but could hardly have expected $100 dollars for her trouble.

She was not alone in being surprised by Benjamin Traoré over the next 24 hours. At 09:00 UTC in Djigouera, Joseph received a call from his bank in Bobo Dioulasso. They had received a transfer into his account of $1,356,412 US from an anonymous donor. The reference on the transfer was 'street boys.' This amount had completely cleaned out Benjamin's current account, which he'd promptly closed.

At 08:00 PST, having failed to receive a response from the wake-up call and under pressure from the driver sent to collect him, the hotel staff entered Benjamin's room. He was sat in the hotel's comfortable working chair at the leather-covered desk. His arms hung behind him, his shoulder blades hooked on the chair back; his chin pointed to the ceiling. The top of his head was missing and his new shiny revolver lay on the plush carpet below his lifeless right hand.

The room was quite a mess.

Although he would never know from whence it came — in fact he wondered if it was from one of his fellow CaMPuS Directors who was less than happy with his leadership — Casper opened a beautifully gift wrapped parcel. It was full of cow excrement and came with an exquisitely gilded and embossed card bearing the legend, "Somebody somewhere thinks you're a shit".

Somewhat rattled by a pathetic and cowardly gesture of truculence, Casper made his way to the offices of Deaf Cat, via Candice's mom's apartment. He found himself whistling as he drew up outside, the lightness of his mood not entirely due to the fact that carrying a passenger would allow him to use the pool car lane on the sometimes congested Interstate 5.

On the journey he managed to draw out the recently arrived and heavily culture-shocked Candice on the subject of her beloved Dalit.

He was moved by Prity's story and irritated by the struggle to get HWI personnel to achieve outcomes rather than outputs. He became increasingly angry as he questioned Candice about the lack of civil rights afforded to the Dalit, OBC and Scheduled Caste peoples trapped by a Hindu culture that consigned them to hell on earth.

If he was motivated to get in the game of justice before, he was boiling hot now.

Seeing Laodicea

Bella was delighted to see Candice, cordial towards Casper. Once the greetings subsided to happy smiles, they had a reprise of the conversations so far.

First came a lengthy update on problems solved with the Living Dälight site. There had been a technical glitch around stock updates. It was vital that nothing could be ordered in the USA that was out of stock. If that did happen, any payments taken would need to be refunded and incur a repayment fee. Any items remaining in stock and failing to automatically update could trigger a financial meltdown if large numbers of customers placed orders that could not be fulfilled within the advertised time.

A labelling fiasco had seen an entire consignment of baskets destroyed by US Customs. Although the shipping agent was insured against such a possibility, an investigation was underway that might result in the uncompensated loss of the entire shipment.

Finally, an agent claiming to be a Christian NGO representing Macy's Department Stores had taken a large order of beautiful banana leaf sandals on 90 days' credit and then failed to pay. Having convinced Candice that she was committed to altruistic Christian service, the customer had stolen their sandals. It had been a bitter blow and a salutary lesson. No more trade would be conducted on trust with an apparently sympathetic charitable business.

These early teething troubles had the power to discourage and demotivate the Dälight team. Bella, aware of Candice's near despair, was full of platitudes and unsubstantiated encouragements. Casper was sharper in his questioning about how these things had happened. It was obvious from his manner that he was disappointed that supposedly competent people had failed. He wanted to know what had been done to ensure there would be no repeat of these misfortunes. Bella rolled her eyes and ignored him, except to point out acidly that the web glitch was minor, easily fixed and a result of the irritating but unavoidable presence of human beings involved in the processes. No, she would not be writing a procedure or drawing up non–conformance reports.

Labels falling off, which declared a product's country of origin, was a more difficult issue to solve. It was somewhat dependent on the customs officer's approach to testing the permanence of the labelling. A detailed report was filed by the shipping agent, which confidently stated that the unpicking tool used by an undoubtedly churlish officer would be unable to repeat the problem in future.

The meeting finally turned to its main topic — campaigning for social justice.

Casper brought a presentation prepared by his team. It was not particularly artistic, something Bella noted with some disdain. It did however neatly explain the early wins or "low hanging fruit" which had already been made.

'We have three celebrities willing to donate their services as models for our campaign. They are prepared to sign agreements that they will never model products from any other source than Transparent Trade or their authorised partners."

When she heard the list, two of whom she had met, Bella was somewhat skeptical that Casper could make the agreements stick.

'Why would Pamela Bell and Martha Bennett, both married to high profile NFL players, want to get involved in this?'

'Their husbands both played in the Aztecs team with me back at SDSU. Both couples attend churches similar to mine. We went out together as friends a few weeks back and while the two girls have modelling pasts, neither particularly wants a standard career in modelling. Their celebrity is far more developed and their direction of travel is away from fashion not towards it. They are interested only in the publicity their involvement will generate, and both feel a strong commitment to our cause. Their husbands are willing to strut about in our stuff too, though they may need a little help in how to stand and smile and do whatever models do.'

Bella bridled a little at Casper's rather dismissive approach to what she knew to be a highly competitive, skilled and professional discipline. She was excited to meet these celebs though, especially as she would have to meet the challenges of getting a cohesive message through the lens — out of fairly inexperienced but highly attractive people. She was full of ideas already and naturally keen to look at what existing sportswear manufacturers' contracts affected these four high-profile individuals.

'Why have you gone for church attenders?' Bella asked. 'I can just imagine how a poster full of Mormon haircuts and jackets will go over.' She was quick to send a pointed remark at the immaculately tailored and well-barbered Casper.

'Hey you and your girlfriend might have more in common than you think with a sex cult like the Mormons!' Casper was straight back with a cheap shot.

'Easy you two. Bella, Casper and I can't help the fact that there can be an oxymoron to be found in the term Christian fashion. Hopefully we and Casper's friends are exceptions to your rules.

'Casper, if you think Bella's sexual preferences are the only defining properties worth using in cheap comebacks, it probably says a lot about the way you see her, and therefore about your own prejudices. You could quite easily have stuck with how she dresses, there's enough material there for you to work with.' She was pleased with the emphasis on the word material.

'Now put the guns away and wait for an enemy to draw them on cowboys.'

The meeting accelerated as the natural frissons of worldview clashes receded, and the obvious strengths of conviction, commercial acumen and communications expertise found one another once more.

Four hours later, they headed for a restaurant, and continued their discussions late into the night. It was a tremendously important evening; one that allowed Casper to reveal how exposed and friendless he was as Chairman of CaMPuS — possibly not for much longer. It was Bella who, after 45 minutes of intense questioning, threw him the communications lifelines he would need to extricate himself. She explained the need to rebuild trust regarding his competence. She held that he was in possession of all necessary top cards to see off the challenges ahead.

She advised that he should remind the board that from the outset, the business had been established around his particular skills at delivering projects. He was the success at the heart of CaMPuS' achievement. He should challenge the team to put up a candidate that could lead them to a brighter future, based upon their personal delivery of the main thrust of the business.

Too many lesser players were taking for granted the strength of the great ones — without whom they would have no context for their minor contributions. She was certain — absolutely certain that he could win that dogfight.

Once back in the ascendency he should explain the importance of millennial thinking and its increasing interest in ethics.

'The future is ethical. Take the team back to revisit core values that you established, probably on the back of an envelope when there were just four or five of you, all kids, trying to get going. You're all grown up now and it's time to get some grown up principles. This is your opportunity to establish an ethical essence to which your people must align.'

Candice and Casper, though tempted to crash at Bella's place, slipped away very late in the Porsche and raced back towards San Diego. Their heads were full of vision; the plans for a steady build towards a shock and awe marketing campaign for Transparent Trade fairly advanced.

Seeing Laodicea

Even with an initially fairly modest scale of product, they would be able to begin influencing public perception of brand, value, quality and injustice. Their twin aims of changing the fortunes of large numbers of families trapped by poverty, and forcing the clothing industry to clean up its social justice act would run and build in parallel. Conversation in the car was excited, Casper was pumped.

It was around Carlsbad that Casper was pulled over by a Highway Patrol officer, on account of the speed at which his vehicle was travelling. The subsequent arrest, booking and charge for DUI followed on swiftly. Candice completed the journey by taxi, Casper spent the night in a cell.

24. GOODBYES

Casper cried — howled actually — openly, publicly for the first time in many years. He was back at Mission Hills Christian Community Fellowship. Along with everyone else in the congregation, he was processing the announcement that had carefully been read by Faye's dad. Her dad had insisted on doing this himself, a point of honour for a man whose strength had been most severely tested by watching his beloved daughters struggle together to deal with the terrible progress of ALS in the love of his youngest's life. He and his wife had been a constant, intelligent, spiritually alert and caring support to the whole family. They had done their best. But it had not been enough to save Chip, only God could do that and he seemed to be saying 'No.' By any measure, it had been an incredible effort.

Faye had confided to him that her sister Joy had been a rock, her 'go to' player in a wonderful team of friends. The piece he read singled Joy out for appreciation, among the many others who had been intrinsically involved. This team, some of whose lives had been suspended over the past few weeks, had stood around the little family shoulder to shoulder. Within this ring of loving support, Chip's condition had collapsed to the point where he reluctantly clung to life by a thread, in constant pain. His endurance had been both wonderful and terrible to behold. His dignity and care for the feelings of those around him — utterly exemplary. It was hard to imagine anyone dying better.

The church congregation had been praying, fasting, pleading with God for a reverse in the illness. It was almost unbelievable to some that the Almighty had not relented in the face of such overwhelming pressure.

Even now, when the damage ALS had done to Chip appeared irreversible, many prayed every day for his healing and restoration. It came as a shock therefore to the worshippers to hear Faye's dad read the final words of his script.

'Chip and Faye have asked that members of the church change the focus of their prayers from healing to release.'

The worship leader took the meeting forward from there, verbalising the thoughts of many.

'This is a morning where tears are entirely appropriate.'

Casper bawled.

The same morning up in Los Angeles International Airport, Candice sat quietly in her economy seat on Qatar Airways. Preparing for the long flight to Istanbul she gratefully accepted the hot wipe from an attentive cabin steward. There had been a substantial delay in loading the aircraft and she was one of many passengers feeling tense, anxious to be away.

She glanced out of her circular window, allowing her gaze to be briefly diverted by the prismatic effect of the pane's thickness.

The unmistakable shape of a coffin could clearly be seen being lifted into the hold by the baggage handling machine. On the top of the coffin the simple label read 'Benjamin Traoré — Ouagadougou.' The coffin was of a reasonable standard. The travel insurance company had refused any liability on account of Mr. Traoré's death being at his own hand. Repatriation and funeral costs were being picked up by United Medical. One final nail in the coffin, so to speak, of his reputation, was that he had died without discernible assets. All of his properties were rented. Even the bank account that received his salary was empty, and he had recently been paid. No claim could be made on his estate.

'Poor man,' Candice thought, supposing that he had died in the States while on holiday. She was slightly disconcerted to think of a corpse travelling a few feet beneath her. Putting the morbid thought out of her mind, she busied herself choosing music and browsing the in–flight film menu for anything she'd not already seen. She had read good things about The Butler, and Saving Mr. Banks. Depending on how much Kindle reading and sleep she could manage, she thought it might be possible to see them both in the 20 hour journey ahead.

She had much to arrange on arrival. It would be a matter of weeks before Casper touched down in Ahmedabad, by which time she and Prity would need all the necessary meetings lined up. Finances for Dälight were in horrible deficit, despite the best efforts of Lifted Sister, Bella's web team and the US direct sales operations at Living Dälights. But despite the financial pressures, all of the artisans and Indian staff team had been properly paid by Dalight. Everyone else was either a volunteer or a drain on the reserves propped up by Casper's donations. Candice's services were gratis, courtesy of her financial supporters.

According to Prity there were pleasing signs among the artisans that fair pay was beginning to show its transforming effect. Her hard working friends who ran and contributed to the cooperative and small business suppliers of Dälight were able to improve their housing. Children were starting to attend schools and medical treatments were being purchased. Life, for the extremely poor was hardly a bowl of cherries, but no longer a bitter struggle.

Candice had gone through the financials with Casper, and he was happy that the all–important cash flow line was moving steadily towards health. If their insurance claim for the stock destroyed by US Customs was paid, and the debacle with the fraudulent "Macy's" agent hadn't happened, they would by now be starting to show a modest profit.

But it wasn't the limited, though healthy operations of Dälight that occupied the majority of Casper's time. He was much more focused on the establishment of production for Transparent Trade. Bella had connected him to a clothing buyer of considerable skill and excellence. Bella's friend would be accompanying him on his trip to India.

Casper had made contact himself with a couple of investigative journalists linked to Human Rights Watch in order to meet and retain their services. He needed reliable, libel suit proof information. In view of the battles ahead, if incorrect or unverifiable information somehow fed into Transparent Trade's publicity machine, they would not survive a law suit any more than Lynx had when the fur trade closed in. He would be meeting journalist contacts based in Asia while on his trip to India.

Casper was also bringing a small team of contractual experts from CaMPuS. Following the almost unanimous backing of the shareholders in an extraordinary meeting called by the board, a couple of key resignations had made room for new, more altruistic blood in the boardroom to replace that which had been spilled on the carpet.

Bella had been right. When questioned on whether the company was prepared to ditch its most precious asset, everyone had backed down. The attempt to force Casper to change course had called on him to show his hand, which was stacked with aces. No Casper, no CaMPuS; they would go with his more ethical approach. He had two years to demonstrate that ethical and profitable could become bedfellows.

Casper's team was tasked with setting in place bespoke premises to house elite and well-compensated production and management teams.

He would want an operation as slick and tidy as any that constructed his weapons systems. Wherever he built a production unit, Casper was committed to providing English speaking schools for the children of his workers, adult education classes for the workers themselves and their wider family, and health clinics — all of which would be subsidised and affordable for employees.

There was a lot to organise: the construction of HR systems that would embed robust grievance procedures — including out of country whistle–blowing functions to combat the possibility of caste partiality. A positive discrimination recruitment policy in favour of those on or below the scheduled caste stratum of the cultural hierarchy would be rigorously implemented. A mixed management economy of local and ex–pat collaboration would operate until such time as full ownership could transfer to Gujarat.

Candice and Prity were to be assigned key oversight roles on HR, ethos and employee engagement. As she tensed through the rapid acceleration of take–off, trying to ignore her neighbour's halitosis problems, Candice offered silent prayers of gratitude for the provision of the whirlwind that was Casper Alexander Scales.

Following his rather shamefaced call upon returning from Carlsbad police station, they had enjoyed a number of meetings. Throughout the remainder of her stay in San Diego, he had made office space for her at the CaMPuS HQ premises — which had blown her mind when she'd first seen them.

The Porsche had been exchanged for an impressive BMW, and an intern had appeared on the staff team as Casper's driver. One man's DUI charge was another man's opportunity to pick up an incredible company car and climb the first rung on an employee ladder that was stretched upwards stratospherically.

In something of a cliché, their last evening together had seen Casper make one despairing pitch for changing the level of their relationship.

'Candice, will you marry me?'

Seeing Laodicea

He made his request from one knee, at the 94th Aero Squadron restaurant, astonishing ring in open case, huge bouquet standing by.

It had been an impressive offer, and one made from a man who had clearly become a kindred spirit. Candice surprised herself with her answer.

Casper's emotional exposure was experiencing a month of extremes. He was tasked with working on the presentation sequence for Chip's funeral. Faye picked out the photographs and video sequences she most wanted included. Casper, eyes filled with tears, went through the pictures, cut them into categories and interspersed them with title pages styled like silent movie dialogue stills. This last act of service for his friend needed to be delivered to the high standards Chip himself would have presented with.

The whole sequence was timed to fit the 3 minutes and 39 seconds of Faye's chosen backing track God's Great Dance Floor and concluded with some delightful video of the family laughing and playing.

Chip was carried into the church on the shoulders of his gaming friends. Each one wore a purple and black striped tie; representative of the colour of Chip's board game pieces. He was always purple or black. The friends also wore brightly coloured socks, each the colour of their own favourite game piece.

The funeral began with the presentation sequence through which most sobbed. Fabulously, Faye made three contributions. The first was certainly the most punishing. She chose to play Vera Lynn's Smile, When Your Heart is Breaking, standing looking at the packed congregation impassively, with a most generous smile of appreciative remembrance, without comment.

Her second piece was a song sung in her nightingale voice, with just the hint of a quiver from time to time. What was most audible

258

was her heart full of faith in her God who said no. Broken yet strong.

Finally she gave her tribute to an exceptional man, who became great through suffering.

'I grieve today for two men. The first, the man I married, a good-looking man whose beauty and exceptional talent caused me to fall instantly in love with him.

'The second, and on reflection the one I loved the most, was the man he became through the progression of his illness. A human being of such dignity and courageous love, that my proudest moments came with when he was most broken.'

Later, as family and friends stood around the grave looking down at the lowered coffin, having each tossed in a single rose in turn; it fell to Casper to pray over their friend, colleague, lover, son, father.

'Lord, we remember that a long time ago your friends and family stood around your grave to say goodbye to you. The reason for our hope today is that death could not keep you and the grave could not hold you.

'We entrust to you our friend Chip, sharing with you the grief of our loss, taking comfort in these circumstances from the one who said, "I am the resurrection and the Life, whoever believes in me, shall live, even though he dies."

'If you had uttered those words and not risen from the grave, we would have no basis for our hope. But we have read the accounts of reliable men who went to their deaths declaring that you did indeed rise from the dead. We, like they, have experienced for ourselves the transforming power of the Holy Spirit, and as did Chip in incredible ways during his darkest moments. We rely on the cross of Christ to do all that is legally necessary to deal with our sin and failure. We have confidence in your power to do for Chip what you said you will do for those who place their trust in you.

Seeing Laodicea

'We look forward to being reunited with him. In the meantime we declare our determination to live our lives in such a way that will please you to identify with us — whom you have adopted to carry your name and your reputation to the ends of the earth.'

As the prayer ended Casper looked into the damp eyes of those at the grave. He was committed to the struggle for social justice and was excited to follow the way in which his desire to be a disciple of Christ was leading him. However, nothing in his experience to date had shaped him quite as profoundly as becoming part of Chip's caring family. If anyone had asked Chip, 'Where's God in this?' — Referring to the dreadful suffering and terrifying, pitiless, unremitting progress of his illness, he would have replied without hesitation, 'In my family and my friends.'

Casper realised at that moment that his friend, whose body he had learned to treat as his own, had gifted him with something very special.

'I am proud to be a part of the family of God; to play my part in manifesting the values and principles of the Kingdom — whose coming was announced by Jesus Christ during his ministry on earth and whose advance has been entrusted to its members.

'I too am ready to die well — if necessary an untimely death of suffering — if that is what is required of me.'

He smiled through humbled tears, looking down one last time upon the flower–strewn coffin, grateful.

POSTSCRIPT

So my friend, we have taken a little time together to explore something of the sadly real matters of exploitation, prejudice and religious bigotry that I've chanced upon around the world. Hopefully, while that was going on, you noticed the amazing, courageous and genuinely loving actions of some of my other friends. Yes, as you may have guessed, much of the book is real, and many of its characters are out there, right now, doing incredible things to change the lives of others for the better. One of them said this to me recently: 'We only truly develop maturity of character and in personal spiritual growth when we give ourselves to help others.'

All the while, I hope you kept in mind the clothing you yourself were wearing. We did mention it right back at the beginning.

This brings me to a rather delicate matter. You see, unless you have thoroughly and intentionally engaged in eliminating from your life any complicity with exploitation, you have most likely benefitted from the suffering of others in the act of getting dressed today (if you are dressed — some people read in the bath I'm told.)

Just after putting the final full stop (that's a period to US readers — we don't mention those over here) on the last paragraph of the main body of the text, I ran into some friends whose daughter was graduating from studying fashion design. She was involved with an initiative called Visible Clothing, crowdfunded in 2014. As I investigated, I was amazed at how very like our fictional Transparent Trade this organisation turned out to be.

Visible Clothing was born in the aftermath of the tragic, deadly collapse of the Rana Plaza[1] on 24 April 2013 killing 1129 people employed in garment manufacture and injuring over 2000 more. Visible's two founders, Andy Showell–Rogers and Andy Lower, reviewed their wardrobes and threw out every item of clothing that they could not guarantee had been produced by people treated well. They ended up rather naked. You can watch their story on the Visible website: visible.clothing

Visible is committed to finding ways of linking customers like you to fairly produced garments. They are not alone, I picked them out because of their rather engaging story. I guess if I listed all the others, the list would quickly date and you might feel I was patronising you. You know what to do if you want to trade ethically.

So let's wrap up (see what I did there?) with a final glance at your wardrobe. I suspect that you and I both sometimes present ourselves formally in the presence of God, or Dad as he prefers to be known, to let him know how much we love him or share a few concerns, maybe ask him for things.

It may come as a shock to both of us to realise that he comments on what the citizens of Laodicea are wearing when he's conducting an audit on their progress as a church — all recorded in the New Testament book of Revelation. Isn't he supposed to be a benevolent old kingly figure rather than some kind of investigator? Can't we expect him not to look too closely, or at least not to make comment on shortcomings? Apparently not.

---

[1] Extract from Wikipedia, to remind ourselves of what this was:
    It is considered the deadliest garment–factory accident in history, as well as the deadliest accidental structural failure in modern human history. The building contained clothing factories, a bank, apartments, and several other shops. The shops and the bank on the lower floors immediately closed after cracks were discovered in the building. Warnings to avoid using the building after cracks appeared the day before had been ignored. Garment workers were ordered to return the following day and the building collapsed during the morning rush–hour.

In the light of this 'revelation,' I wonder what he thinks of us when we turn up for an audience with him? Would he comment on our fine designer garments, or would he see through the cut of our jacket to the label, and beyond it to those who made it, and what it was made of and how that was produced? Would he notice that the suppliers were attractive to us because they kept their costs down by using trafficked children as slave labour? Would it matter to him that the fabric was dyed at great cost to the environment, somewhere where it doesn't matter because we don't live there?

How embarrassing to have made purchase choices based on trampling the poor or wrecking 'our' planet!

But shopping ethically or not is one small part of a busy life isn't it? So easily our every waking moment can disappear into a variety of potentially embarrassing things. Embarrassing that is when we are in conversation with the risen Jesus.

Let's start with our commitment to structures with values designed to perpetuate or increase injustice. Maybe we commit to them so that we can earn our wages or perhaps because they have persuaded us that they make legislative decisions in our interest.

Added to our contractual and voting commitments, what about the tendency within our cultures to invest vast amounts of time and energy in pursuit of insatiable consumerist desires. Finally, if we are to avoid awkwardness in the presence of Jesus we would do well to check out any fear, prejudice and self–interest dominated relationships with those of different backgrounds.

The list of personal compromises and regretful acts of selfishness is unique to each of us but has a disappointing familiarity for many.

Jesus sees right through all that, and we stand before him exposed.

So what can possibly clothe us there? How can we avoid an appraisal that includes words like these?

'You say "I am rich, I have everything I want, I don't need anything!" And you don't realise you are poor and wretched, miserable and naked and blind.'

Oh dear, look at those last two words: naked and blind!

Well I have a theory. Acts of obedience emanating from a loving relationship with Jesus clothe us in righteousness. His righteousness, gifted by him to us by including us in his amazing, wonderful work of renewal. Those who want to relate to him can do so by merit of his gracious adoption at tremendous cost, into his family. Having joined the family, there's plenty to do, and that brings me to a final update.

Readers of Touching Smyrna may be interested in learning how things have progressed with the Kodeni School Project featured in its postscript.

Well, a very mixed company of 26 Europeans and one American raised around £60,000 — some of it from you, readers of Touching Smyrna, but mainly from their own pockets and those of their friends. One couple gave up all their wedding presents, asking for cash gifts to be given to the school fund instead. I have encountered such generosity at funerals (no flowers, gifts to Hospice / Air Ambulance etc.) but never before at a wedding — extraordinary.

The people on and around the team went without what they wanted in order to be part of the answer to over ten years of prayer by those in need of outside help.

The Kodeni School team travelled to Burkina Faso in February 2015 and grafted in the hot red dirt, alongside a huge number of new Burkinabe friends. Together they built the foundations of the first half of the much-needed school. They also committed themselves to fund the building of a well, in due course.

In a couple of short years their project will meet the two most pressing needs of the next generations of villagers in Kodeni: clean water and good quality primary education. If you missed the boat on helping them with funds, why not go to the aidtoburkina.co.uk website and take it from there? There's another half to build yet.

I have spoken with many of the team members since their experience. They have used expressions like 'truly alive' and 'incredible sense of self-worth' to describe what it was like to give up time, money, comfort and inactivity for a sacrificial and highly challenging effort. Maybe in spending themselves on those trapped by poverty, they gained true riches? Perhaps they responded intuitively to Jesus' words to the church at Laodicea, 'Come and buy gold from me.'

Perhaps you have had similar experiences yourself as you have elected to do something sacrificial for someone, finding in your own growth of character and wellbeing, true riches. Especially when it got really hard. Possibly even in reading this, you're developing more of an appetite for justice and righteousness in your life. I think Jesus mentions that too, elsewhere:

'Those who hunger and thirst for righteousness will be satisfied.'

Maybe the members of the Kodeni school team aren't quite as naked in the presence of Jesus as they would have been before.

He gets all the credit — after all, he's the one who adopted them — shared his family values with them. He empowered them to make good choices, cared for them, shared the journey, laughed and cried with them as they went about his business.

Like we said, he gets all the credit, but they get to wear his clothes.

Kodeni School Team, February 2015

aidtoburkina.org.uk

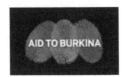

Made in the USA
Charleston, SC
28 July 2016